Knitting Never Felt Better

the definitive guide to fabulous felting

Nicky Epstein

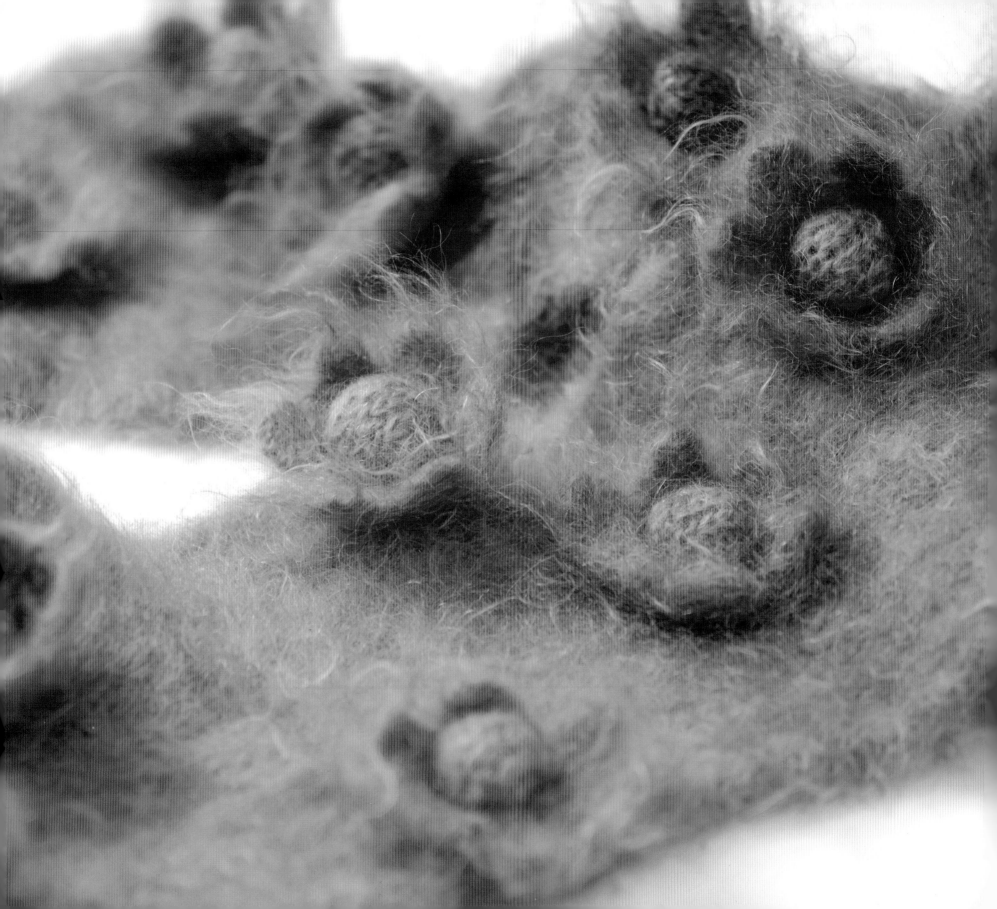

Knitting Never Felt Better

the definitive guide to fabulous felting

Nicky Epstein

sixth&spring books

sixth&spring
books

Vice President, Publisher
TRISHA MALCOLM

Editorial Director
ELAINE SILVERSTEIN

Art Director
CHI LING MOY

Book Division Manager
ERICA SMITH

Associate Editors
ERIN WALSH
AMANDA KEISER

Yarn Editor
TANIS GRAY

Instructions Editor
EVE NG

Instructions Proofreader
SUSAN HAVILAND

Copy Editors
KRISTINA SIGLER
MARJORIE SINGER ANDERSON

Graphic Designer
SHEENA T. PAUL

Production Manager
DAVID JOINNIDES

Photography
JACK DEUTSCH STUDIOS

President, Sixth&Spring Books
ART JOINNIDES

Library of Congress Control Number: 2006932952
ISBN: 1-933027-11-8
ISBN 13: 978-1-933027-11-1

1 3 5 7 9 10 8 6 4 2
Manufactured in China

First Edition

introduction

WARNING: Felting is addictive. Those of you who have felted before know what I mean. Those of you who have not should be prepared to embark on a wondrous new knitting experience that may change you from a docile, contented, traditional knitter into…a wildly creative felting freak! So don't say I didn't warn you.

Felting is a process that turns knitted wool into matted wool through the alchemy of hot water and agitation. The transformation is exciting, chic, adventurous, challenging, magical and creatively inspirational. You will produce knitted pieces you've never even dreamed of before that will astound you and those around you. Your friends—and total strangers—will ask questions like "Wow, how did you do that?" You will knit original pieces and transform them into objects that are totally new and bold; you will find yourself seeking out an old sweater at a flea market, felting it and turning it into a beautiful hat, slippers, scarf—anything that your imagination can conjure up. Felting is knitting alchemy: turning ordinary yarn into spun gold.

I accidentally discovered felting years ago when I washed a cherished Aran sweater and it shrank down to munchkin size (we all have "Honey, I shrunk the sweater" stories). I was devastated—I thought it was ruined. Then I noticed the sweater's beautiful new texture. At the time I didn't realize it could have been converted into a magnificent handbag. Now I and thousands of other knitters are shrinking garments on purpose to create fashionable felted treasures.
In this book I will show you a variety of techniques, patterns, projects and tips that make felting such a joy. Your washing machine will become your magic cauldron as you discover that hot water, soap and agitation can be your friends, not your foes. With a little courage and luck, you'll master the process and take your knitting skills and aspirations to new heights. Felting can turn "craft" into "art," and it is fun, fun, fun!

Welcome to the fascinating, wonderful and unpredictable world of felting…and may the gods of the washing machine smile on you and your projects. I think you'll feel as I do…knitting never felt better!

Nicky Epstein

Felting Freak

1
go felt yourself

Felting is the process of turning wool into matted wool. Sound dull? It's not! It's a magical metamorphosis, a fashionable transformation that can turn mundane into magnificent, a road that takes knitters to a whole new world of creativity. All you need is some wool, water, soap, a washing machine, a little imagination, guts…and, oh yes…this book.

I love to felt and I hope you will too. It's chic, exciting, semi-predictable and lots of fun. Felting (sometimes called "fulling") has been around for thousands of years. Initially it was used to make wool into wind- and water-resistant garments. Today, it is enjoying a tremendous renaissance. Wool becomes felt when exposed to hot and cold water, soap, pressure, agitation and friction. And the change is far from subtle.

How does felting work? First of all, untreated wool and other animal fibers (mohair, alpaca, cashmere, angora) will work best. Treated or washable wools (such as Superwash wool) will not felt, but many wool blends will give you interesting results, as long as they contain at least 50 percent natural fiber. Manmade fibers will have to be content to remain in their original state.

Wool fiber is made up of tiny scales. When exposed to hot water, these scales open up and expand, and with the agitation in a washing machine, the fibers rub together and become tightly and irreversibly entangled. The addition of soap helps swell the scales and lubricate the fibers. When the scales are then exposed to cold water, they close down in a tight mesh. That is, they felt! The resulting fabric will look and feel entirely different from the original piece.

HOW DO YOU FELT?

THE FELTING PROCESS

How do I felt? There are a number of ways to do it, including hand felting as our ancestors did (see page 115), but in this book I've concentrated on washing-machine felting, the method that works best for me after much trial and error.

Loosely knit pieces work the best, but normal-gauge knits will felt well too. Generally, it is said that pieces need to be knit very loosely, but I have found that regular knitting felts well. Make a gauge swatch and felt it before beginning your project, especially if you are using a different yarn than the one suggested.

Before felting, put the knitted pieces in a mesh laundry bag to avoid tangling, to keep small pieces together and to reduce the amount of lint left in the washer. (Mesh bags come in many sizes—choose one that fits your project comfortably.) Set the machine on the hot wash/cold rinse cycle, set the water level as low as possible, and add a small amount of liquid soap. Top-loaders give you more control because

they allow you to lift the lid and check the piece during the felting process, but front-loaders work too. In fact, I have used a front-loader for many of the projects in this book. I like to throw an old pair of jeans in with the piece to increase the agitation. Some people use old sneakers or towels. I don't recommend using towels, because lint can work its way into the felted piece.

If you use a top-loading washing machine you can closely watch the progress by stopping the machine every few minutes and removing the garment to check it, until you have achieved the desired effect. You may find that the piece is felted after two or three minutes, or you may have to repeat the agitation cycle. For most of the projects in this book, complete felting requires an entire agitation cycle, or even two or three repetitions of the cycle. For many projects, especially those that don't have to fit, such as handbags and pillows, you can let the washing machine do the work of spinning and rinsing. Remove the piece as soon as the spin cycle ends to avoid creasing.

If a piece has to fit, or if you don't want to lose your stitch pattern, such as for lace or cables, watch the piece carefully as you're felting. If you remove the piece before the spin cycle, rinse it in cold water, then gently roll it in a towel to remove excess water. Finally, hand-shape it flat or on a mold (for example, use a bowl to produce a round shape) and let it thoroughly air dry. How quickly it will dry depends on whether you let it go through the spin cycle or took it out wet, and of course on the humidity and temperature of the drying room.

Results will vary depending on how your washing machine agitates, whether you have hard or soft water, the kind of soap you use, and of course the yarn itself. Even the color can be a factor—some white or light-color yarns will not felt. Do a test swatch first, until you become more comfortable with the process. Soon you'll be an expert, although the somewhat unpredictable nature of felting, along with the experimentation the process invites, is part of the fun. And, start with easy projects.

good yarns: top ten yarns for felting

In preparing this book I asked sixty yarn shop owners around the country about their favorite felting yarns. Here are the results, in alphabetical order:

Brown Sheep Company **Lamb's Pride**

Cascade Yarns **220**

Crystal Palace Yarns **Iceland**

Knit One, Crochet Too **Paint Box**

Noro/Knitting Fever, Inc. **Kureyon**

Manos del Uruguay/Design Source **Handspun Semi-Solids**

Plymouth Yarn Co. **Galway**

Reynolds/JCA **Lopi**

Nashua.Handknits/Westminster Fibers Inc. **Creative Focus**

Shetland-type wools (for example, Harrisville Designs)

But many other yarns (including those that I've used in this book) work wonderfully as well. Find your own favorites.

Felting FAQs

Any questions so far? Fire away! Here are a few that I am most frequently asked.

Q: How much does the yarn shrink?

A: A general rule is that the knitted piece will shrink by about one-third. See the pictures on the following pages to see how some different yarns react. However, every yarn will react differently—that's why a swatch is a valuable tool to show how the yarn will perform. It will give you a good idea of the outcome, but keep in mind that a larger piece might react somewhat differently than the swatch. Some items, like scarves, may actually get longer during felting. Monitoring the piece in the washer will give you the result you desire.

Q: Will the colors fade?

A: Some fading may occur, but this is part of the charm of felting. Again, the swatch will show you the final result. To be safe you can add ½ cup of vinegar or more to the wash water, depending on the size of your project.

Q: Should I felt all the pieces of my project at the same time?

A: Yes, if you want uniformity. Each wash cycle can produce different effects, even with the same yarn. In fact, in most cases assembling the main pieces of your project before felting will give you the best results.

Q: How and when can you tell if a project is felted enough?

A: One of the nicer aspects of felting is how personal the process is. You decide when your project is felted enough. Generally speaking, felting is complete when the stitches and stitch patterns disappear, but you call the shots by staying on top of the process. If you want the stitch patterns to remain visible, stop the process sooner. The swatches on the following pages show you how different fibers react to felting. Chapters 2, 3 and 4 show you what happens to different types of knit stitches during felting.

Q: What if the felt shrinks too much?

A: Uh-oh! Unfortunately, there is no turning back. But see Chapter 6, Cut It Out!, for projects to make out of pieces of felted knitting.

Q: Do pattern stitches work?

A: Stockinette and garter stitch are best suited for felting, because most stitch patterns are lost in the process. However, in Chapters 3 and 4 you'll find a selection of stitches that offer some alternatives. Shorter felting times can preserve some stitch patterns like cables or lace.

Q: Is there a way to keep edges from ruffling or curling?

A: Baste your edges before felting. Sew a running stitch with a cotton thread. To keep bag openings from ruffling, stitch them together before felting. Remove the thread after felting is complete.

Q: What kind of soap should I use and how much?

A: Liquid laundry detergent (without bleach). Use ¼ to ½ cup depending on the project size. Some felters use dish washing liquid. It also works, but use less.

before and after

The following pages show how different natural fiber yarns of different weights react to felting. I used a wide selection of fibers, including wool, mohair, silk, angora, alpaca and cashmere, and I knit all the swatches in stockinette stitch, casting on 22 stitches and working 40 rows. Each photo shows one unfelted swatch and one felted so you can see the "before and after" effect of the process. In all cases, I used needles two or three sizes larger than those recommended on the yarn label. Each photo caption tells you the yarn's name and fiber content and how many times I ran it through the wash cycle to felt it. These pictures will help you understand how felting affects yarn and what you can expect to happen to your knitted pieces during felting.

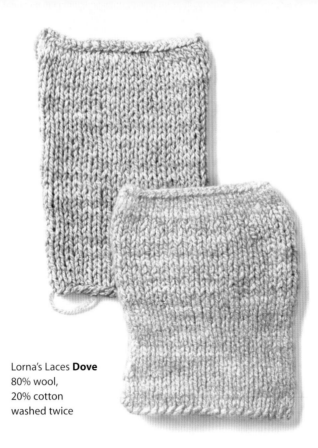

Lorna's Laces **Dove**
80% wool,
20% cotton
washed twice

Lorna's Laces **Angel**
70% angora, 30% lambswool
washed twice

Lorna's Laces **Glory**
mohair blend
washed twice

Lorna's Laces **Grace**
mohair blend bouclé
washed once

Lorna's Laces **Heaven**
90% kid mohair,
10% nylon
washed once

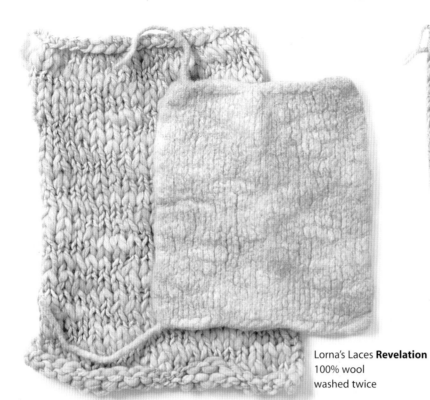

Lorna's Laces **Revelation**
100% wool
washed twice

Lorna's Laces **Fisherman**
100% wool
washed twice

Lorna's Laces **Helen's Lace**
50% silk, 50% wool
washed once

Lorna's Laces **Lion and Lamb**
50% silk, 50% wool
washed twice

Lorna's Laces **Bullfrogs and Butterflies**
85% wool, 15% mohair
washed twice

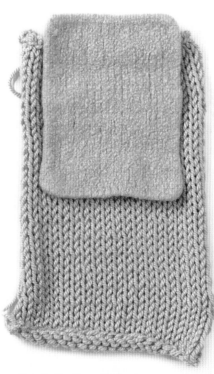

Trendsetter Yarns **Kashmir**
65% cashmere, 35% silk
washed twice

Nashua Handknits/
Westminster Fibers Inc.
Painted Forest
100% wool
washed twice

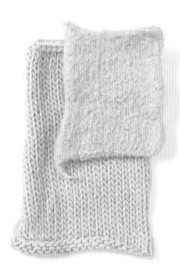

Nashua Handknits/Westminster
Fibers Inc. **Creative Focus Worsted**
75% wool, 25% alpaca
washed twice

Plymouth Yarn Co. **Indiecita Alpaca Sport**
100% alpaca
washed twice

Plymouth Yarn Co. **Baby Alpaca Worsted**
97% baby alpaca, 3% stellina
washed once

Plymouth Yarn Co. **Baby Alpaca DK**
100% superfine baby alpaca
washed once

Plymouth Yarn Co. **Alpaca Bouclé**
90% alpaca, 10% nylon
washed twice

Plymouth Yarn Co. **Baby Alpaca Grande**
100% superfine baby alpaca
washed once

Plymouth Yarn Co. **Baby Alpaca Brush**
80% baby alpaca, 20% acrylic
washed twice

tip

Waste not, want not! Use your swatches to make iPod and cell phone cases. And, if you are making a bag, use them as pockets.

chic mock tweed hat

Use a beautiful handpainted wool to create a tweed effect in this stylish, easy-to-knit hat.

FINISHED MEASUREMENTS

Before felting

Approx 34"/86.5cm circumference x 16"/40.5cm H

After felting

Approx 20"/51cm circumference x 10"/25.5cm H

MATERIALS

• 2 3½oz/100g balls (approx 66yd/60m) Plymouth Yarn Co. **Handpaint Wool** (wool) in #190 camouflage

• Size 17 (12.5mm) needles

• Circular option: Size 17 (12.5mm) 16" circular needle and/or set of dpns.

GAUGE

7½ sts and 10 rows = 4"/10cm over St st using size 17 (12.5mm) needles.

HAT

Cast on 70 sts. Work in St st for 5½"/14cm.

Dec row 1 (RS) *K1, k2tog; rep from *, end k1—47 sts.

Cont in St st until piece measures 13½"/34.5cm from beg.

Dec row 2 (RS) *K1, k2tog; rep from *, end k2—32 sts.

Work in St st for 4 rows, rep Dec row 2—22 sts.

P 1 row.

Next row *K2 tog; rep from * to end— 11 sts.

Last row *P2tog; rep from *, end p1— 6 sts.

Pass first 5 sts over last st. Fasten off. Sew seam

Circular option

With circular needle or dpns, cast on 70 sts. Pm and join for working in the round.

Work in St st (k every rnd) for 5½"/14cm.

Dec rnd 1 *K1, k2tog; rep from *, end k1—47 sts.

Cont in St st until piece measures 13½"/34.5cm from beg.

Dec rnd 2 K1, *k1, k2tog; rep from *, end k2—32 sts.

Note Change to dpns when needed. Work in St st for 4 rnds, rep Dec rnd 2— 22 sts.

P 1 rnd.

Next rnd K1, *k2tog; rep from *— 11 sts.

Last rnd *K2tog; rep from *, end k1— 6 sts.

Break yarn and thread tail through rem 6 sts. Fasten securely.

Felt according to instructions on p. 8. Fit on head while damp and shape brim as pictured.

vase/needle holder

FINISHED MEASUREMENTS

Before felting

Approx 20"/51cm H x 15"/38cm diameter (base)

After felting

Approx 13"/33cm H x 10"/25.5cm diameter (base)

MATERIALS

- 1 1¾oz/50g ball (approx 55yd/50m) of Lion Brand Yarn's **Landscapes** (wool/acrylic) in #275 autumn trails
- Size 11 (8mm) needles
- 1 wine bottle for shaping
- Glass pebbles

GAUGE

10 sts and 15 rows = 4"/10cm over St st on size 11 (8mm) needles before felting.

VASE

Starting at the top, cast on 30 sts. Work in St st, inc 1 st each side every 6th row 4 times—38 sts. Work even until piece measures 20" from beg, end with a WS row.

Shape base

Row 1 (RS) *K2, k2tog; rep from *, end k2—29 sts.

Rows 2 and 4 Purl.

Row 3 *K2tog; rep from *, end k1—15 sts.

Row 5 *K2tog; rep from * to end—8 sts.

Row 6 [P2tog] 4 times—4 sts.

Slip 2nd, 3rd and 4th sts over first st.

Fasten off leaving a long tail. Sew seam. Felt according to instructions on p. 8. Slip over wine bottle while damp and shape neck. Remove bottle and reshape. Let dry completely. Place glass pebbles in vase to keep upright.

On to the next chapter—Dimensional Felting. There I'll demonstrate the ancient Japanese shibori process, giving it a few new twists of my own. I'll also show you some fascinating three-dimensional effects you can achieve through the magic of felting. It just gets more and more amazing—and more fun!

2
dimensional felting

Dimensional felting is like performing a magic trick: A piece of plain, flat stockinette stitch takes on a three-dimensional quality. You perform this sleight of hand by inserting a shrink-resistant object into the piece before felting.

The first example of dimensional felting I ever saw was a scarf in the American Folk Art Museum in New York, and I was fascinated with its unique beauty. The background was felted, and its surface was covered with integrated balls that were not felted and that had visible stitch patterns. After some thought, I realized that the way to achieve this effect was to insert round, unshrinkable objects into the knitted piece, hold them in place with rubber bands, felt the piece and then gently remove the rubber bands and inserts. The rest of the piece would felt, but the parts fastened around the unshrinkable objects would not. I tried it, and the results were spectacular. I later discovered that this was a Japanese technique called shibori.

When I looked for round objects to use, the first ones I thought of were marbles. Strangely enough, marbles are not easy to find in New York City. I experimented with many unshrinkable objects that varied in size and shape. Some worked and some did not, but my passion for the technique grew.

In this chapter, I'll share with you what did work, and you'll see what great fun it is. With a few basic, easy-to-find materials, you'll become an expert on dimensional felting. Marbles, nuts, Ping-Pong balls, glass pebbles, seashells, wooden balls, sticks, golf balls—they'll all work! You can buy many of these things at your local crafts store or find them on a walk in the park or along a beach. Take any of these shrink-resistant items, secure them with rubber bands into your knitted piece in a pleasing pattern, and felt. In addition to the shibori-type patterns, this chapter includes a wide selection of dimensional stitch patterns that felt well.

dimensional techniques old and new

❶ This swatch is knitted in seed stitch. Before felting, I secured large and small marbles in place with rubber bands.

❷ This time, I used stockinette stitch and inserted only small marbles, placed close together.

These swatches are knitted in stockinette stitch. I inserted wooden balls instead of marbles.

❸ The stripes were done by alternating two rows of dark pink acrylic yarn with two rows of light pink wool.

❹ Wooden balls were inserted only on the edge.

For these swatches, I used small marbles in clusters.

❶ This is what the swatch looks like after felting but before I removed the marbles.

❷ Marbles used to form an edging.

❸ Marbles and rubber bands have pulled the fabric into folds.

❹ For this swatch, I used different-size balls to form a diagonal pattern.

❺ These before-and-after photos show large marbles placed in a mohair swatch.

ball cape

The dimensional effect achieved through use of the shibori technique enhances the beauty of this mohair cape.

FINISHED MEASUREMENTS
Before felting
Approx 27½"/70cm W x 105½"/268cm L
After felting
Approx 16"/40.5cm W x 42"/106.5cm L

MATERIALS
• 10 1¾ oz/50g balls (approx 98yd/90m) Nashua Handknits/Westminster Fibers, Inc. **Creative Focus Kid Mohair** in #17 aqua
• Size 10½ (6.5mm) needles
• 72 2"/5cm to 2½"/6.5cm balls (for example: Ping-Pong balls, golf balls, wood dowel caps, walnuts) and rubber bands

GAUGE
14½ sts and 21 rows = 4"/10cm in St st on size 10½ (6.5mm) needles before felting

CAPE
Note Cape is worked from side to side.
Cast on 40 sts. Working in St st, inc 1 st at beg of every row until there are 100 sts. Work even in St st until piece measures 94"/239cm from beg. Cont in St st, dec 1 st at beg of every row until 40 sts rem. Bind off.

Insert balls, placing 38 balls evenly around edge of cape and 22 balls randomly at center.

Front ties (make 2)
Cast on 14 sts. Work in St st for 60"/152.5cm. Starting at one end, insert 6 balls in each tie 5"/12.5cm apart.

FINISHING
Felt according to instructions on p. 8. Let dry thoroughly before removing rubber bands and balls. Sew plain ends of ties to upper edges of fronts.

angel puff scarf

This ethereal scarf knits up quickly and uses exactly one skein of yarn. Make one or several in the colors of your choice.

FINISHED MEASUREMENTS
Before felting
Approx 9"/23cm W x 49"/124.5cm L
After felting
Approx 4"/10cm W x 32"/81.5cm L

MATERIALS
• 1 .88oz/25g ball (approx 229yd/207m) Rowan **Kidsilk Haze**
(mohair/silk) in #581 Meadow OR #633 Violetta OR #592
Heavenly
• Size 6 (4.25mm) needles
• 4 dozen hazelnuts and rubber bands

GAUGE
Approx 20 sts and 26 rows = 4"/10cm in St st using size 6
(4.25mm) needles

SCARF
Cast on 45 sts. Work in St st until ball is finished, leaving enough
to bind off. Bind off.

FINISHING
Insert 24 hazelnuts randomly over 12"/30.5cm at each end of
scarf. Felt according to instructions on p. 8.,
placing scarf in laundry bag.
Let dry throughly before
removing rubber
bands and nuts.

tip

This
scarf is knitted
out of fine yarn with
small needles. If you have
a knitting machine,
now is the time
to use it!

❶

ping-pong balls

❶ Two-color mohair background with Ping-Pong balls centered on the color change.

combination technique

❷ This swatch shows two techniques used in combination: glass pebbles inserted before felting, and a metal binder clip clamped on while the piece was drying to create a ruffled edge.

tip

The smaller the rubber band, the easier it is to wrap and unwrap the nuts. Small rubber bands can be found in beauty supply stores.

❷

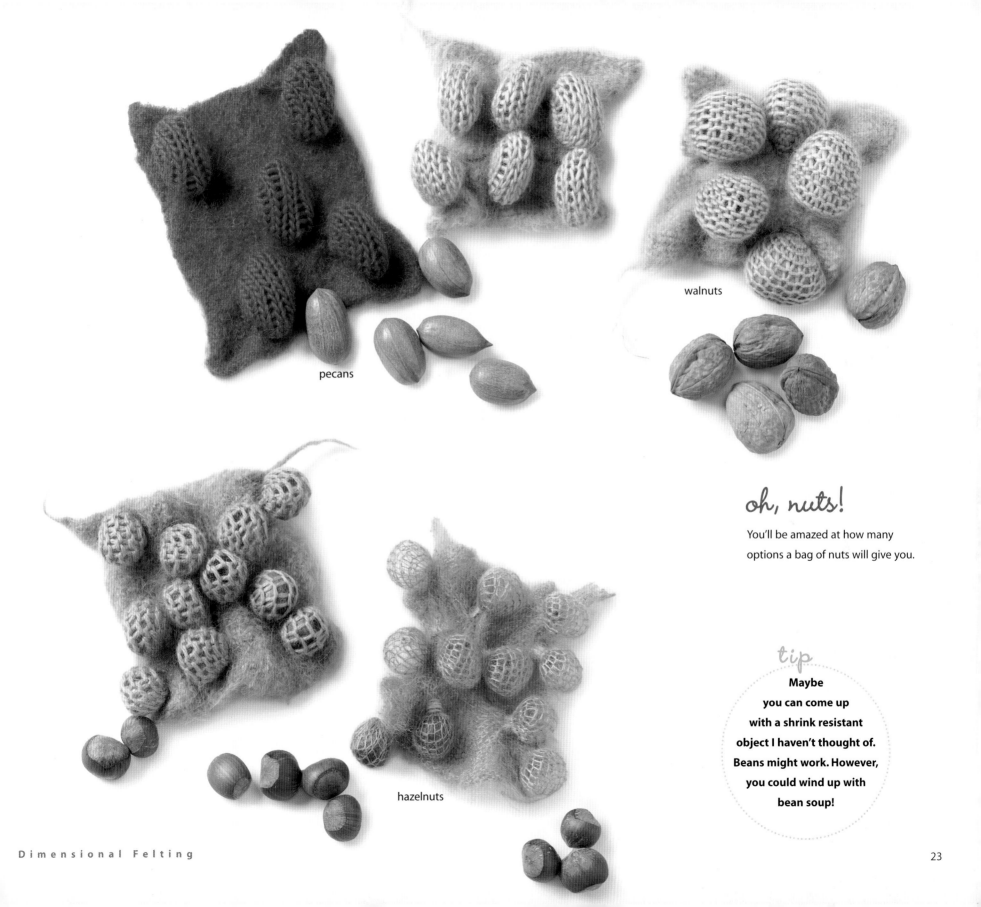

pecans

walnuts

hazelnuts

oh, nuts!

You'll be amazed at how many options a bag of nuts will give you.

tip

Maybe you can come up with a shrink resistant object I haven't thought of. Beans might work. However, you could wind up with bean soup!

holiday trees

Create a magical holiday with these ethereal trees. Vary the texture by using mohair for some trees and an angora blend for others.

FINISHED MEASUREMENTS

Right: Classic Elite Yarns
La Gran
Before felting
Approx 12"/30.5cm H x 13.5"/34.5cm circumference (at base)
After felting
Approx 8½"/21.5cm H x 10"/25.5cm circumference (at base)

Left: Tahki Yarns/Tahki•Stacy Charles, Inc. **Jolie**
Before felting
Approx 18"/45.5cm H x 11.5"/29cm circumference (at base)
After felting
Approx 12½"/32cm H x 9"/23cm circumference (at base)

MATERIALS
• 1 1½ oz/42g ball (approx 90yd/82m) Classic Elite Yarns **La Gran** (mohair/wool/nylon) in #6501 bleached white
• Size 9 (5.5mm) needles
• 42 small marbles and rubber bands

• 1 .88oz/25g ball (approx 108yds/99m) of Tahki Yarns/Tahki•Stacy Charles, Inc. **Jolie** (angora/ wool) in #5001 white
• Size 7 (4.5mm) needles
•60 small marbles and rubber bands

Purchased gold stars and bead trim for decoration

GAUGE
Approx 16 sts = 4"/10cm over St st using **La Gran** and size 9 (5.5mm) needles.
Approx 20 sts = 4"/10cm over St st using **Jolie** and size 7 (4.5mm) needles.

TREES
Directions are written for **La Gran** (Jolie).
Cast on 53 (57) sts. Work in St st for 6½ (10½)"/16.5 (26.5)cm.
Dec row *K2tog; rep from *, end k1—27 (29) sts.
P 1 row.
Work in St st for 4½ (6)"/11.5 (15)cm.
Rep dec row—14 (15) sts.
P 1 row.

Next row *K2tog; rep from *, end k0 (1)—7 (8) sts.

Angora tree only
P 1 row.
Dec row *K2tog; rep from * to end—4 sts.
Last row [P2tog] twice—2 sts.

FINISHING
Cut yarn leaving a long tail. Thread tail through rem sts, pull tightly and secure. Sew seam. Insert marbles randomly over surface of tree. Felt according to instructions on p. 8, placing tree(s) in a laundry bag. Let dry thoroughly before removing rubber bands and marbles. Make cardboard cones to fit under your trees or purchase Styrofoam cones from a craft store. The trees may also fit over bottles.

tip

Subtle multicolor yarns also make lovely trees. When using angora or mohair, use a hair dryer on the finished tree to create a fluffier look.

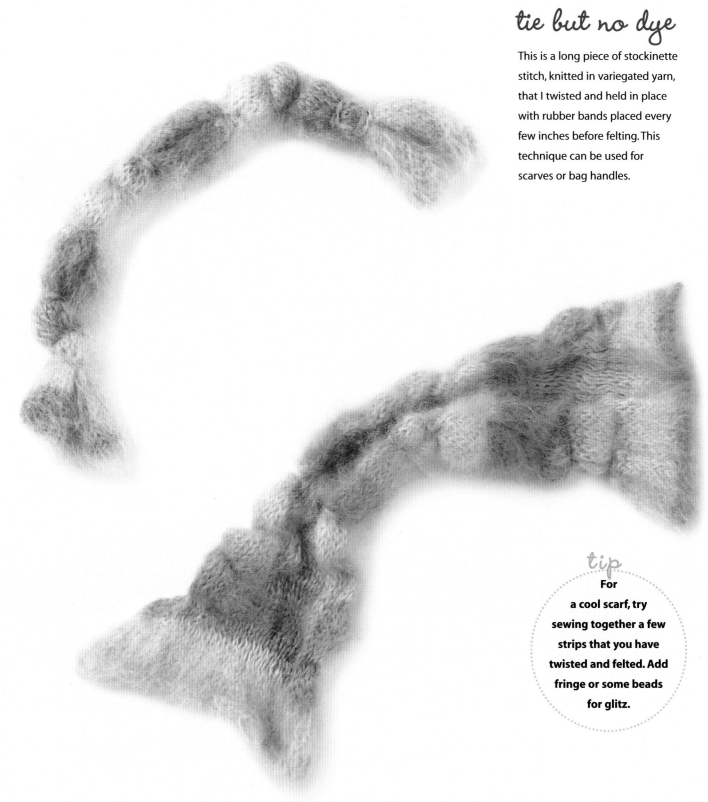

tie but no dye

This is a long piece of stockinette stitch, knitted in variegated yarn, that I twisted and held in place with rubber bands placed every few inches before felting. This technique can be used for scarves or bag handles.

tip

For a cool scarf, try sewing together a few strips that you have twisted and felted. Add fringe or some beads for glitz.

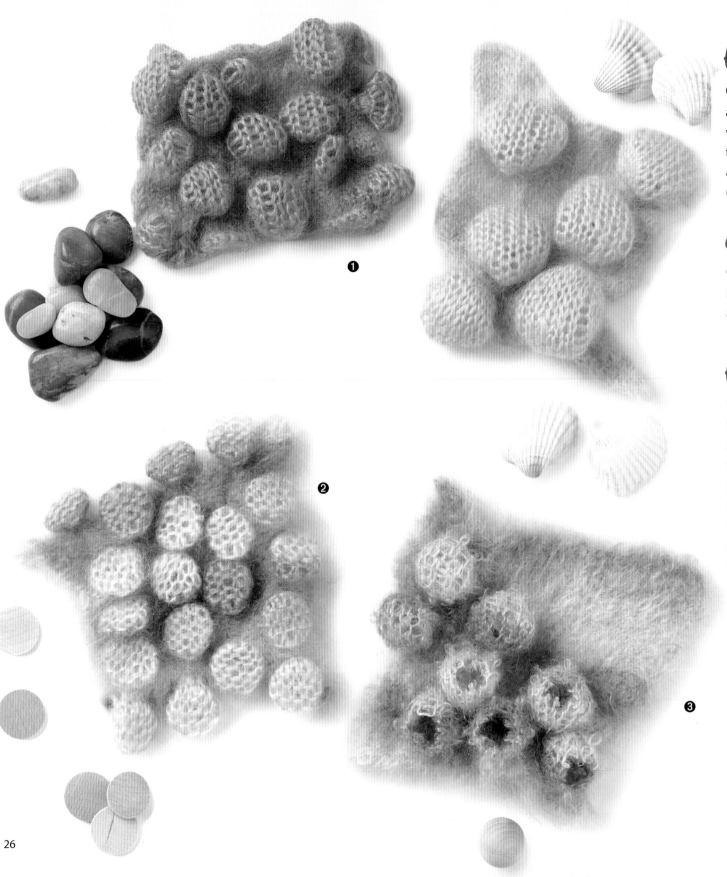

found objects

❶ These swatches show how you can achieve different effects by using a variety of objects. Maybe you can find your own unique objects in addition to pebbles and shells like I've used here.

discos

❷ Wooden discs are placed together in an overlapping pattern, creating attractive clusters.

floradoras

❸ I used a multicolor bouclé yarn for the background and set the wooden balls in loosely so the bouclé would felt a little around the balls and the yarn fibers would tangle. After the swatches were felted and dried, I removed the rubber bands and balls and gently snipped the top of each round shape to create a flower.

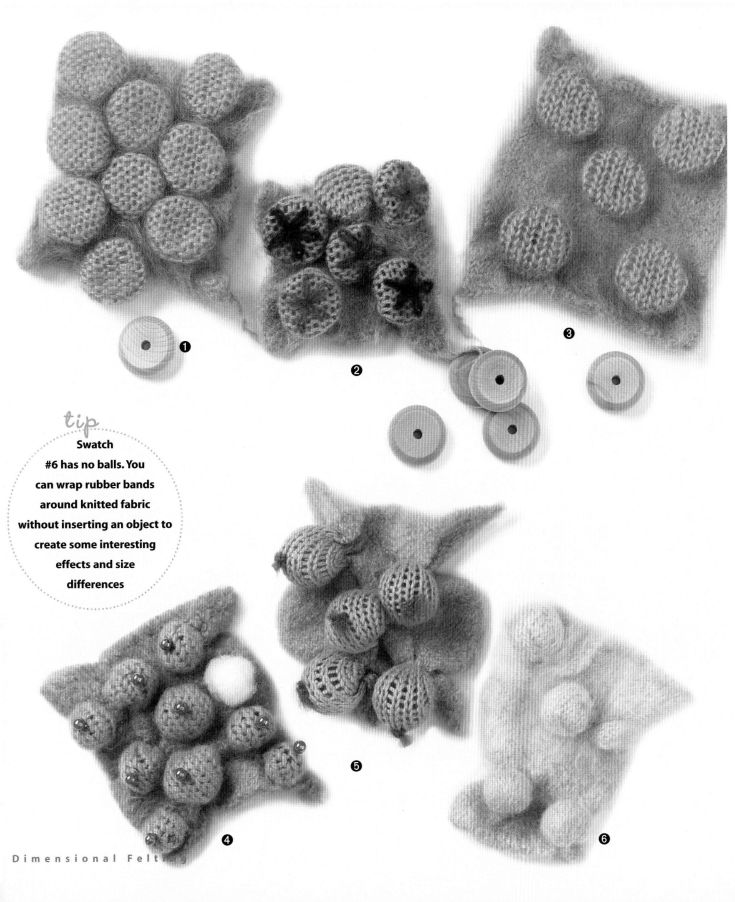

For these swatches, I used flat wooden disks and mohair yarn.

❶ Disks inserted very close together on a reverse stockinette stitch background.

❷ Floral embroidery done before felting on a reverse stockinette background. (See Techniques for embroidery stitches).

❸ Disks spaced further apart on a stockinette background.

❹ I used fiberfill here to make different-size balls. The advantage of using fiberfill is that you can leave it in after the piece is felted. Be careful not to overstuff, or the fill will show through. After the piece was felted, I sewed a bead to the tip of each ball.

❺ Tipped balls. After the ball is inserted, tie a triple knot fringe about 2" long to the tip of each ball. After the piece is felted, cut the fringe short.

❻ No balls. This swatch was knitted with wool on the bottom half and mohair on the top half. After knitting, I secured parts of the knit fabric with rubber bands. During felting, the fabric shrank to form the balls.

tip
Swatch #6 has no balls. You can wrap rubber bands around knitted fabric without inserting an object to create some interesting effects and size differences

daisy-stitch beauty

❶ These photos show before and after felting. After inserting the balls (I used small wooden balls here), I embroidered a daisy around each ball about ¼ inch from the rubber band (see Techniques). This left room for the ball to pop out after felting.

berry clusters

❷ Again, these are before-and-after swatches. I inserted hazelnuts to form the berry cluster and sewed on knitted leaves before felting. See page 29 for leaf pattern.

berry nice scarf

You'll feel berry, berry nice when you wear this lovely mohair scarf embellished with shibori berry clusters and knitted leaves.

FINISHED MEASUREMENTS
Before felting
Approx 12"/30.5cm W x 52"/132cm L
After felting
Approx 7"/18cm W x 40"/101.5cm L

MATERIALS
• 3 1½ oz/42g balls (approx 90yd/82m) Classic Elite Yarns **La Gran** (mohair/wool/nylon) in #6541 cape cranberry (MC)
• 1 ball each #6539 eucalyptus green (A) and #6572 underappreciated green (B)
• Size 10 (6mm) needles
• Tapestry needle
• 41 hazelnuts and rubber bands

GAUGE
16 sts = 4"/10cm over St st using size 10 (6mm) needles before felting.

SCARF
With MC, cast on 48 sts. Work in St st until piece measures 52"/132cm from beg.
Bind off.

LEAF (make 4 each in A and B)
Cast on 5 sts.
Row 1 (RS) K2, yo, k1, yo, k2—7 sts.
Row 2 and all WS rows Purl.
Row 3 K3, yo, k1, yo, k3—9 sts.
Row 5 K4, yo, k1, yo, k4—11 sts.
Row 7 Ssk, k7, k2tog—9 sts.
Row 9 Ssk, k5, k2tog—7 sts.
Row 11 Ssk, k3, k2tog—5 sts.
Row 13 Ssk, k1, k2tog—3 sts.
Row 15 SK2P—1 st.
Fasten off.

FINISHING
Insert nuts foll photo.
Sew one A and one B leaf at the top of each cluster. Felt according to instructions. Let dry thoroughly before removing rubber bands and nuts.

> **Don't be afraid to insert the nuts near the edges. Curvy irregular edges give any piece a unique fashionable look.**

3-d floral

❶ These before-and-after shots show a technique for creating beautiful three-dimensional flowers. Knit the outer flower separately (see p. 31) and sew it in place after securing the wooden balls. Sew the flower loosely about ¼" out from the rubber band. This will leave room for the ball to pop out after felting.

sweethearts

❷ I found these glass hearts in a flower shop. Wooden hearts from a craft shop would work just as well. This technique is shown after felting.

❶

❷

2-in-1 floral scarf

Because of the magic of felting, you can create two entirely different scarves with the same pattern just by varying the yarn. Even though both scarves are made of mohair/wool blends, the two yarns felted differently, resulting in two scarves of varying sizes and very different looks.

FINISHED MEASUREMENTS

Before felting

Both yarns: Approx 11"/28cm W x 82"/208.5cm L

After felting

Lorna's Laces **Glory**: Approx 7½"/19cm W x 68"/172.5cm L

Plymouth Yarn Co. **Outback Mohair**: Approx 5½"/14cm W x 60"/152.5cm L

MATERIALS

- 4 2oz/57g skeins (approx 120yd/110m) Lorna's Laces **Glory** (mohair blend) in #50ns poppy

OR 2 3½ oz/100g skeins (approx 218yd/196m) Plymouth Yarn Co. **Outback Mohair** (mohair/wool/nylon) in #801 green/blue/grey

- Size 10 (6mm) needles
- Tapestry needle
- Sixteen 1"/2.5cm wood dowel caps and rubber bands

GAUGE

16 sts and 20 rows = 4"/10cm over St st using size 10 (6mm) needles before felting.

SCARF

Using provisional cast-on (see Techniques), cast on 43 sts. Work in St st until piece measures 82"/208.5cm from beg.

Carefully remove provisional cast-on, placing sts on needle. With RS facing, join yarn and work fringe.

Fringe

Bind off 2 sts, *sl st back to LH needle, cast on 5 sts, bind off 7 sts; rep from * to end. Fasten off.

Flower (make 16)

Cast on 6 sts.

Rows 1–3 Knit.

Row 4 Sl 1, k3, with LH needle lift 2nd, 3rd and 4th sts over first st, k2—3 sts.

Row 5 Knit.

Row 6 Cast on 3 sts, k to end—6 sts.

Rep rows 1–6 five times more.

Bind off. Sew last bound-off edge to cast-on edge for 3 sts starting at center.

FINISHING

Insert dowel caps as pictured. Place a flower over each wrapped cap approx ½"/.5cm from rubber band and sew loosely to the knit fabric over the cap. Felt according to instructions (see page 8). Let dry thoroughly before removing rubber bands and dowel caps.

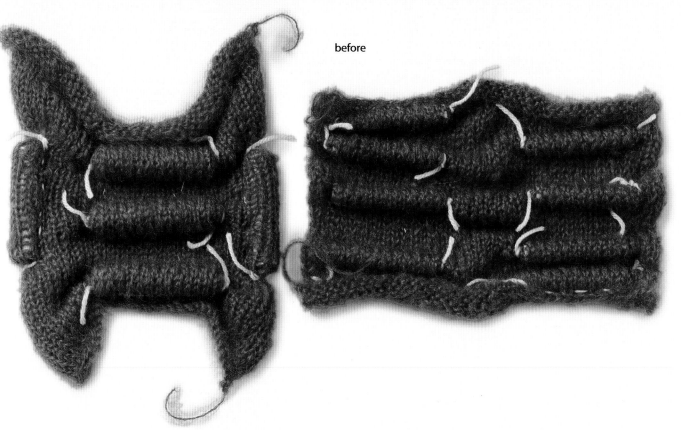

wooden dowels

Here I've used wooden dowels cut into short lengths and arranged them in various patterns. Sew the dowels in place before felting with acrylic or cotton thread. Make sure to sew all ends in securely so the dowels don't slip out during the rough felting process. After felting, cut the threads out very carefully and remove the rods.

after

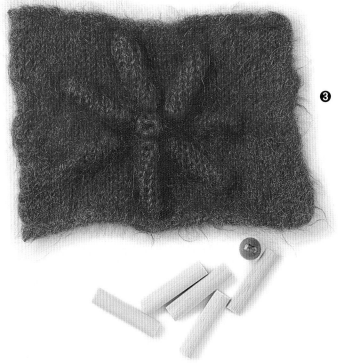

three stages of a swatch

❶ I used pins to mark the placement of the dowels.

❷ Dowels and marble secured in place.

❸ Felted flower

dowel ribs

❹ **Row 1 (RS)** *K3, p3, rep from *, end k3.
Row 2 (WS) *P3, k3, rep from *, end p3.
Rep rows 1 and 2 for desired length.

Before felting, place cut dowel rods into the ribs on the WS as shown. Sew securely all around each rod. After felting, remove stitches and rods.

before

after

get a grip!

You can use metal clamps to achieve interesting dimensional effects. The shaping takes place after felting. While the piece is still wet, use metal clamps to create welts or curves. You may have to move the clamps around while the piece is drying to achieve smooth curves. These before-and-after photos show some possibilities.

crystal and pearl

This is a prime example of a dramatic felting change.

❶ (multiple of 10 sts plus 2)

Rows 1 and 2 Purl.

Row 3 (WS) Knit.

Row 4 *K1, [yo, ssk] 3 times, k1; rep from * to end.

Row 5 and all WS rows Purl.

Row 6 *K2, [yo, ssk] twice, k2; rep from * to end.

Row 8 *K3, yo, ssk, k3; rep from * to end.

Row 10 Rep row 6.

Row 12 Rep row 4.

Rep rows 1–8.

Insert Ping-Pong balls before felting.

bubble wave

I felted this two-color textural pattern both with and without inserts (hazelnuts in this case) to show the different effects you can achieve with the same stitch pattern.

❷ Colors A (dark) and B (light)

(multiple of 22 sts plus 4)

Rows 1 and 3 (RS) With A, knit.

Rows 2 and 4 With A, purl.

Row 5 With B, k2, *k7, turn, sl 1 wyif, p2, turn, sl 1 wyib, k4, turn, sl 1 wyif, p6, turn, sl 1 wyib, k8, turn, sl 1 wyif, p10, turn, sl 1 wyib, k21; rep from *, end k2.

Row 6 With B, k2, *k11, p11; rep from *, end k2.

Rows 7–10 With A, rep rows 1–4.

Row 11 With B, k13, *k7, turn, sl 1 wyif, p2, turn, sl 1 wyib, k4, turn, sl 1 wyif, p6, turn, sl 1 wyib, k8, turn, sl 1 wyif, p10, turn, sl 1 wyib, k12; rep from *, end k2.

Row 12 With B, k2, *p11, k11; rep from *, end k2.

Rep rows 1–12.

stringed beads

These before-and-after swatches demonstrate another way to combine shibori technique with a stitch pattern.

(multiple of 10 sts plus 4)

Row 1 (RS) P4, *k1, p4, yo, k1, yo, p4; rep from * to end.

Row 2 K4, *yo, p3, yo, k4, p1, k4; rep from * to end.

Row 3 P4, *k1, p4, yo, k5, yo, p4; rep from * to end.

Row 4 K4, *yo, p7, yo, k4, p1, k4; rep from * to end.

Row 5 P4, *k1, p4, yo, k9, yo, p4; rep from * to end.

Row 6 K4, *p2tog, p7, p2tog tbl, k4, p1, k4; rep from * to end.

Row 7 P4, *k1, p4, SKP, k5, k2tog, p4; rep from * to end.

Row 8 K4, *p2tog, p3, p2tog tbl, k4, p1, k4; rep from * to end.

Row 9 P4, *k1, p4, SKP, k1, k2tog, p4; rep from * to end.

Row 10 K4, *p3tog, k4, p1, k4; rep from * to end.

Row 11 P4, *yo, k1, yo, p4, k1, p4; rep from * to end.

Row 12 K4, *p1, k4, yo, p3, yo, k4; rep from * to end.

Row 13 P4, *yo, k5, yo, p4, k1, p4; rep from * to end.

Row 14 K4, *p1, k4, yo, p7, yo, k4; rep from * to end.

Row 15 P4, *yo, k9, yo, p4, k1, p4; rep from * to end.

Row 16 K4, *p1, k4, p2tog, p7, p2tog tbl, k4; rep from * to end.

Row 17 P4, *SKP, k5, k2tog, p4, k1, p4; rep from * to end.

Row 18 K4, *p1, k4, p2tog, p3, p2tog tbl, k4; rep from * to end.

Row 19 P4, *SKP, k1, k2tog, p4, k1, p4; rep from * to end.

Row 20 K4, *p1, k4, p3tog, k4; rep from * to end.

Rep rows 1–20.

Insert Ping-Pong balls before felting.

pink puff bag

This pretty pink bag knits up quickly in superbulky yarn and big needles.

FINISHED MEASUREMENTS

Before felting
Approx 12"/30.5cm H x 20"/51cm W

After felting
Approx 8"/20.5cm H x 14"/35.5cm W

MATERIALS

• 3 3½oz/100g balls Nashua Handknits/Westminster Fibers, Inc. **Equinox Stripe** approx 66yd/60m (wool/acrylic) in #101 smooch
• Size 17 (12.5mm) knitting needles
• Twelve 1"/2.5cm diameter wood dowel caps and rubber bands
• One Leisure Arts **Exclusively You** 27" moc croc purse handle

GAUGE

7½ sts and 11 rows = 4"/10cm in St st using size 17 (12.5mm) needles.

BAG

Cast on 40 sts. Work in St st until piece measures 33" from beg. Bind off.

FINISHING

Fold fabric to form bag, leaving an 11"/28cm flap. Sew side seams. Mark 12 evenly spaced points on flap ½"/1.5cm from bottom edge and 2½"/6.5cm from side edges. Insert a wood dowel cap at each point.

Felt bag according to instructions.

Let dry throughly before removing rubber bands and dowel caps. Sew handle to each side at seam.

dimensional stitch patterns

This section is a collection of bold textural stitch patterns, such as bobbles, counterpanes and some exciting combinations. Because of their depth of texture, they felt beautifully. Note how the knitted bobbles hold their shape during felting.

bold berries

(Over an odd number of sts)

P2sso Pass 2 slipped sts over just made st.

Row 1 (RS) Knit.

Row 2 K1, *[p1, yo, p1, yo, p1] in next st, k1; rep from * to end.

Row 3 Purl.

Row 4 K1, *[sl 2 wyif, p3tog, p2sso], k1; rep from * to end.

Row 5 Knit.

Row 6 K2, *[p1, yo, p1, yo, p1] in next st, k1; rep from *, end k1.

Row 7 Purl.

Row 8 K2, *[sl 2 wyif, p3tog, p2sso], k1; rep from *, end k1.

Rep rows 1–8.

spoke points

❶ This stitch pattern felts into a bold, solid statement.

(multiple of 12 sts plus 1)

Rows 1, 3 and 5 (WS) K1, *yo, k4, p3tog, k4, yo, k1; rep from * to end.

Rows 2, 4 and 6 K1, *yo, p4, p3tog, p4, yo, k1; rep from * to end.

Rows 7, 9 and 11 P2tog, *k4, yo, k1, yo, k4, p3tog; rep from *, end last rep p2tog.

Rows 8, 10 and 12 P2tog, *p4, yo, k1, yo, p4, p3tog; rep from *, end last rep p2tog.

Rep rows 1–12.

Secure with rubber bands before felting. I felted this swatch without inserts.

pine trees and bobbles

❷ (multiple of 12 sts plus 1)

MB (make bobble) K in [front, back, front, back and front] of st, [turn, p5, turn, k5] twice, sl the 2nd, 3rd, 4th and 5th sts over first st.

Row 1 *K1, yo, k1, SKP, k5, k2tog, k1, yo; rep from *, end k1.

Row 2 and all WS rows Purl.

Row 3 *K2, yo, k1, SKP, k3, k2tog, k1, yo, k1; rep from *, end k1.

Row 5 *K3, yo, k1, SKP, MB, k2tog, k1, yo, k2; rep from *, end k1.

Row 7 *K4, yo, k1, SK2P, k1, yo, k3; rep from *, end k1.

Row 8 Purl.

Rep rows 1–8.

bobble squares

❶ (Worked over 49 sts)

Cast on 49 sts.

Rows 1 and 2 Knit.

Row 3 K2, *MB, k3; rep from *, end MB, k2.

Rows 4 and 6 K2, p to last 2 sts, k2.

Row 5 Knit.

Row 7 Rep row 3.

Rows 8, 9 and 10 Rep rows 4, 5 and 6.

Row 11 K2, MB, k3, MB, k to last 7 sts, MB, k3, MB, k2.

Rows 12 and 14 K2, p to last 2 sts, k2.

Row 13 Knit.

Rows 15–22 Rep rows 11–14 twice.

Row 23 K2, MB, k3, MB, k11, MB, [k3, MB] 3 times, k11, MB, k3, MB, k2.

Rows 24 and 26 K2, p to last 2 sts, k2.

Row 25 Knit.

Rows 27–42 Rep rows 23–26 four times.

Rows 43–54 Rep rows 11–14 three times.

Rows 55–59 Rep rows 3–7.

Rows 60 and 61 Knit.

Bind off.

nosy stripes

❷ Colors A (dark) and B (light) (multiple of 6 sts plus 3)

Cast on with A.

Preparation row (WS) Knit.

Row 1 With B, k1, *sl 1 wyib, k2, [k1, yo, k1] in next st, k1, [turn, p5, turn, k5] twice, k1; rep from *, end sl 1 wyib, k1.

Row 2 With B, k1, *sl 1 wyif, k1, p2tog, p1, p2tog tbl, k1; rep from *, end sl 1 wyif, k1.

Rows 3, 5 and 7 With A, k3, *sl 3 wyib, k3; rep from * to end.

Rows 4 and 6 With A, k3, *sl 3 wyif, k3; rep from * to end.

Row 8 With A, k3, *p3, k3; rep from * to end.

Row 9 With B, k4, *sl 1 wyib, k2, [k1, yo, k1] in next st, k1, [turn and p5, turn and k5] twice, k1; rep from *, end sl 1 wyib, k4.

Row 10 With B, k4, *sl 1 wyif, k1, p2tog, p1, p2tog tbl, k1; rep from *, end sl 1 wyif, k4.

Rows 11, 13 and 15 With A, k6, *sl 3 wyib, k3; rep from *, end k3.

Rows 12 and 14 With A, k6, *sl 3 wyif, k3; rep from *, end k3.

Row 16 With A, k6, *p3, k3; rep from *, end k3.

Rep rows 1–16.

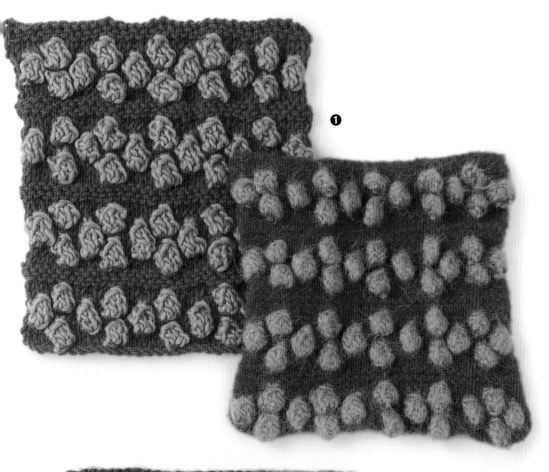

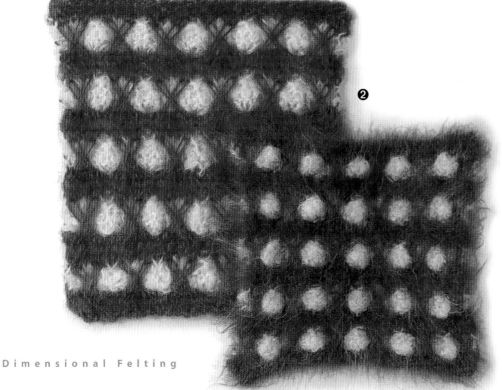

bobbles and ridges

❶ Colors A (background) and B (multiple of 6 sts plus 5)

MB (make bobble) K into front, back and front of next st, turn and p3, turn and k3, turn and p3, turn and SK2P.

Row 1 (RS) With A, knit.

Row 2 With A, purl.

Row 3 K5 A, *MB with B, k5 A; rep from * to end.

Row 4 With A, purl.

Row 5 K2 A, MB with B, *k5 A, MB with B; rep from *, end k2 A.

Rows 6, 7 and 8 Rep rows 2, 3 and 4.

Row 9 With A, purl.

Row 10 With A, knit.

Rep rows 1–10.

snowballs

❷ Colors A (dark) and B (light) (multiple of 5 sts plus 1)

Row 1 (WS) With A, purl.

Row 2 With A, knit.

Row 3 With A, p1, *p1 wrapping yarn twice, p2, p1 wrapping yarn twice, p1; rep from * to end.

Row 4 With B, k1, *sl 1 wyib dropping extra wrap, k2, sl 1 wyib dropping extra wrap, [k1, yo, k1, yo, k1] in next st; rep from *, end last rep k1 in last st.

Row 5 With B, k1, *sl 1 wyif, p2, sl 1 wyif, k5; rep from *, end last rep k1.

Row 6 With B, k1, *sl 1 wyib, k2, sl 1 wyib, p5; rep from *, end last rep k1.

Row 7 With B, k1, *sl 1 wyif, p2, sl 1 wyif, k2tog, k3tog, pass k2tog-st over k3tog-st; rep from *, end sl 1 wyif, p2, sl 1 wyif, k1.

Row 8 With A, k1, *drop first elongated st to front, sl 2 wyib, drop next elongated st to front, with LH needle pick up first elongated st, sl the same 2 sts back to LH needle, then pick up 2nd elongated st onto LH needle, k5; rep from * to end.

Rep rows 1–8.

counterpanes

Counterpanes are richly textured patterns that incorporate cables and lace techniques. Knitted in natural-fiber yarn, they felt beautifully. Knit four or more counterpane squares and sew them together to create a beautiful pillow cover or table mat. I've shown two variations here, but it's fun to find more by searching for historical patterns. Patterns are on p. 44.

quercus leaf

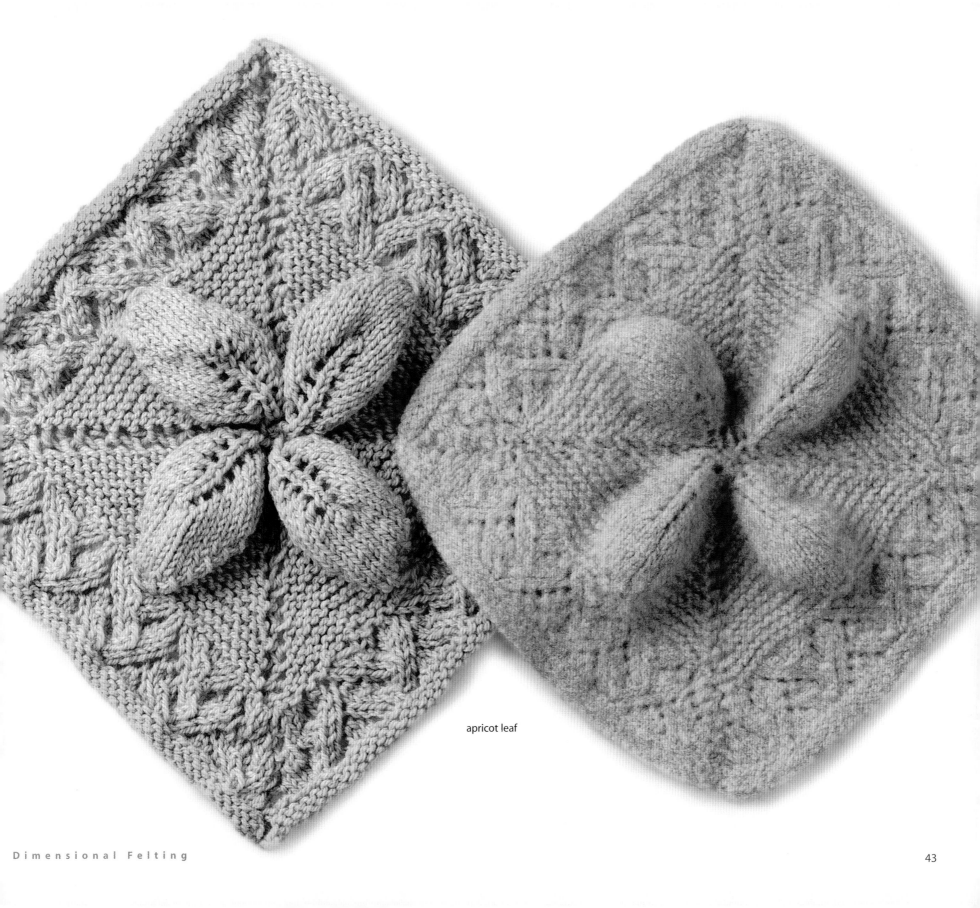

apricot leaf

quercus leaf

Make 4.

Cast on 2 sts.

Row 1 K1, yo, k1.

Row 2 K1, p1, k1.

Row 3 [K1, yo] twice, k1.

Row 4 K1, p3, k1.

Row 5 [K1, yo] 4 times, k1.

Row 6 K1, p7, k1.

Row 7 K1, yo, p1, k2, yo, k1, yo, k2, p1, yo, k1.

Row 8 K1, p1, k1, p7, k1, p1, k1.

Row 9 K1, yo, p2, k3, yo, k1, yo, k3, p2, yo, k1.

Row 10 K1, p1, k2, p9, k2, p1, k1.

Row 11 K1, yo, p3, k4, yo, k1, yo, k4, p3, yo, k1.

Row 12 K1, p1, k3, p11, k3, p1, k1.

Row 13 K1, yo, p4, k5, yo, k1, yo, k5, p4, yo, k1.

Row 14 K1, p1, k4, p13, k4, p1, k1.

Row 15 K1, yo, p5, k6, yo, k1, yo, k6, p5, yo, k1.

Row 16 K1, p1, k5, p15, k5, p1, k1.

Row 17 K1, yo, p6, SKP, k11, k2tog, p6, yo, k1.

Row 18 K1, p1, k6, p13, k6, p1, k1.

Row 19 K1, yo, p7, SKP, k9, k2tog, p7, yo, k1.

Row 20 K1, p1, k7, p11, k7, p1, k1.

Row 21 K1, yo, p8, SKP, k7, k2tog, p8, yo, k1.

Row 22 K1, p1, k8, p9, k8, p1, k1.

Row 23 K1, yo, p9, SKP, k5, k2tog, p9, yo, k1.

Row 24 K1, p1, k9, p7, k9, p1, k1.

Row 25 K1, yo, p10, SKP, k3, k2tog, p10, yo, k1.

Row 26 K1, p1, k10, p5, k10, p1, k1.

Row 27 K1, yo, p11, SKP, k1, k2tog, p11, yo, k1.

Row 28 K1, p1, k11, p3, k11, p1, k1.

Row 29 K1, yo, p12, SK2P, p12, yo, k1.

Row 30 K1, p to last st, k1.

Row 31 K2tog, k to last 2 sts, k2tog.

Row 32 Rep row 30.

Row 33 *K2tog, yo; rep from * to last 3 sts, k3tog.

Row 34 Knit.

Row 35 Rep row 31.

Rows 36–53 Rep rows 30–35 three times.

Row 54 Rep row 30.

Row 55 Rep row 31.

Row 56 P3tog.

Fasten off. Sew rows 1–30 of each square together to form block.

apricot leaf

Make 4.

Cast on 1 st.

Row 1 (WS) [K1, p1, k1] in st.

Row 2 [Yo, k1] 3 times.

Row 3 Yo, k1, p3, k2.

Row 4 Yo, k3, yo, k1, yo, k3.

Row 5 Yo, k2, p5, k3.

Row 6 Yo, k5, yo, k1, yo, k5.

Row 7 Yo, k3, p7, k4.

Row 8 Yo, k7, yo, k1, yo, k7.

Row 9 Yo, k4, p9, k5.

Row 10 Yo, k9, yo, k1, yo, k9.

Row 11 Yo, k5, p11, k6.

Row 12 Yo, k11, yo, k1, yo, k11.

Row 13 Yo, k6, p13, k7.

Row 14 Yo, k13, yo, k1, yo, k13.

Row 15 Yo, k7, p15, k8.

Row 16 Yo, k8, k2tog, k11, SKP, k8.

Row 17 Yo, k8, p13, k9.

Row 18 Yo, k9, k2tog, k9, SKP, k9.

Row 19 Yo, k9, p11, k10.

Row 20 Yo, k10, k2tog, k7, SKP, k10.

Row 21 Yo, k10, p9, k11.

Row 22 Yo, k11, k2tog, k5, SKP, k11.

Row 23 Yo, k11, p7, k12.

Row 24 Yo, k12, k2tog, k3, SKP, k12.

Row 25 Yo, k12, p5, k13.

Row 26 Yo, k13, k2tog, k1, SKP, k13.

Row 27 Yo, k13, p3, k14.

Row 28 Yo, k14, SK2P, k14.

Row 29 Yo, p30.

Row 30 Yo, k2tog, k1, ([yo, k1] twice, SKP, k1, k2tog, k1) 3 times, yo, k1, yo, k2tog, k1.

Row 31 Yo, p32.

Row 32 Yo, k2tog, k1, [yo, k3, yo, k1, SK2P, k1] 3 times, yo, k3, yo, k2tog, k1.

Row 33 Yo, p34.

Row 34 Yo, k4, k2tog, k1, yo, k1, [yo, k1, SKP, k1, k2tog, k1, yo, k1] 3 times, yo, k2tog, k1.

Row 35 Yo, p36.

Row 36 Yo, k2, [yo, k1, SK2P, k1, yo, k3] 4 times, yo, k2tog, k1.

Row 37 Yo, p38.

Row 38 Yo, k4, k2tog, k1, ([yo, k1] twice, SKP, k1, k2tog, k1) 3 times, [yo, k1] twice, SKP, k4.

Row 39 Yo, p40.

Row 40 Yo, k4, k2tog, k1, [yo, k3, yo, k1, SK2P, k1] 3 times, yo, k3, yo, k1, SK2P, k3.

Row 41 Yo, p41.

Row 42 Yo, p42.

Row 43 Yo, k43.

Row 44 Yo, p44.

Bind off. Sew 4 triangles together to form a square before felting.

tip

To maintain the textural beauty of these patterns, use a plain wool yarn and felt lightly. Be careful not to overfelt these.

3
a potpourri of stitch patterns

The stitches most commonly used for knitted fabrics that are to be felted are stockinette stitch and garter stitch. After all, why waste time knitting complicated cables, lace or colorwork when felting blurs stitch definition? But I've experimented with hundreds of stitch patterns that hold their integrity very well in the felting process and allow you to achieve some beautiful and unique effects. In this chapter, I'll show you the cables, mosaics, slip-stitch patterns and lace stitches that work best. I'll also explain how to felt these knitted fabrics and still maintain their visual interest. It's important not to overfelt these pattern stitches, so be sure to read the descriptions that tell you how I made the swatches look the way they do.

cables

Cable patterns can maintain stitch definition when felted, but notice that some actually become wider. These three pairs of swatches, all worked in worsted-weight wool on different needles ranging from size 7 to size 10, show 2 x 2 cables crossed every fourth row. The swatches were put through a hot/cold wash cycle once. Note that they shrank vertically but increased in width. All three show good stitch definition, but if they had been put through another wash cycle, the cables would not be as prominent.

2x2 cable

(multiple of 8 sts)

4-st LC Sl 2 sts to cn and hold to front, k2, k2 from cn.
Rows 1 and 3 (WS) *K2, p4, k2; rep from * to end.
Row 2 *P2, k4, p2; rep from * to end.
Row 4 *P2, 4-st LC, p2; rep from * to end.
Rep rows 1–4.

mixed cable

These swatches were knit in a Shetland-type wool with 2 x 2 cables crossed every fourth row. Needles three sizes larger than those specified on the yarn label were used. The felted swatch endured three wash cycles, which left the cables very subdued.

(multiple of 16 sts)

4-st RC Sl 2 sts to cn and hold to back, k2, k2 from cn.

4-st LC Sl 2 sts to cn and hold to front, k2, k2 from cn.

Rows 1 and 3 (WS) *K2, p4, k2; rep from * to end.

Row 2 *P2, k4, p2; rep from * to end.

Row 4 *P2, 4-st RC, p4, 4-st LC, p2; rep from * to end.

Rep rows 1–4.

3x3 cable

These 3 x 3 cabled swatches were also worked using Shetland-type wool, this time with needles two sizes larger than the yarn band called for. The felted version was put through the hot/cold cycle only twice, so the cables remain prominent.

(multiple of 10 sts)

6-st RC Sl 3 sts to cn and hold to back, k3, k3 from cn.

Rows 1 and 3 (WS) *K2, p6, k2; rep from * to end.

Row 2 *P2, k6, p2; rep from * to end.

Row 4 *P2, 6-st RC, p2; rep from * to end.

Row 5 Rep row 1.

Row 6 Rep row 2.

Rep rows 1–6.

plaited basket stitch

❶ (multiple of 2 sts plus 1)

RT P the 2nd st inserting RH needle from front, p the first st, then sl both sts from needle.

LT K the 2nd st inserting RH needle from back, k the first st, then sl both sts from needle.

Row 1 (WS) P2, *RT; rep from *, end p1.

Row 2 K2, *LT; rep from *, end k1.

Rep rows 1–2, end with row 1.

woven lattice

❷ (multiple of 6 sts plus 2)

4-st LC Sl 2 sts to cn and hold to front, k2, k2 from cn.

4-st RC Sl 2 sts to cn and hold to back, k2, k2 from cn.

4-st LPC Sl 2 sts to cn and hold to front, p2, k2 from cn.

4-st RPC Sl 2 sts to cn and hold to back, k2, p2 from cn.

Rows 1 and 3 (WS) K3, p4, *k2, p4; rep from *, end k1.

Row 2 P1, 4-st LC, *p2, 4-st LC; rep from *, end p3.

Row 4 P3, *k2, 4-st RPC; rep from *, end k4, p1.

Rows 5 and 7 K1, p4, *k2, p4; rep from *, end k3.

Row 6 P3, 4-st RC, *p2, 4-st RC; rep from *, end p1.

Row 8 P1, k4, *4-st LPC, k2; rep from *, end p3.

Rep rows 1–8.

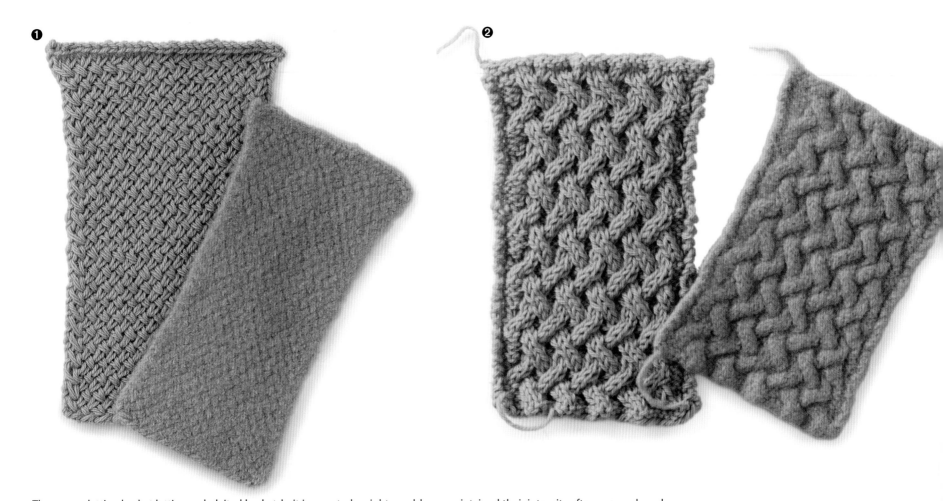

The woven lattice, basket lattice and plaited basket, knit in worsted weight wool, have maintained their integrity after one wash cycle.

basket lattice

(multiple of 8 sts plus 4)

8-st LC Sl 4 sts to cn and hold to front, k4, k4 from cn.

8-st RC Sl 4 sts to cn and hold to back, k4, k4 from cn.

Row 1 and all WS rows K2, p to last 2 sts, k2.

Rows 2, 4, 8 and 10 Knit.

Row 6 K2, *8-st RC; rep from *, end k2.

Row 12 K6, *8-st LC; rep from *, end k6.

Rep rows 1–12.

tip

Do not overfelt these patterns!

mosaics

Mosaics are elegant two-color geometric slip-stitch patterns that use one light and one dark color. They look great both felted and unfelted. The patterns work beautifully for bags, blankets and pillows. I used a lightweight Australian wool and put the swatches through the wash cycle once.

chessboard stitch pattern

Colors A (light) and B (dark)

(multiple of 14 sts plus 2)

Note Sl sts wyib on RS rows, and sl sts wyif on WS rows.

Rows 1 and 2 With A, knit.

Rows 3, 7, 11 and 15 (RS) With B, k1, *k7, [sl 1, k1] 3 times, sl 1; rep from *, end k1.

Rows 4, 6, 8, 10, 12, 14, 16, 20, 22, 24, 26, 28, 30, and 32 With same color as previous row, k all sts worked and sl all sl-sts.

Rows 5, 9 and 13 With A, k1, *[sl 1, k1] 3 times, sl 1, k7; rep from *, end k1.

Rows 17 and 18 With A, knit.

Rows 19, 23, 27 and 31 With B, k1, *[sl 1, k1] 3 times, sl 1, k7; rep from *, end k1.

Rows 21, 25 and 29 With A, k1, *k7, [sl 1, k1] 3 times, sl 1; rep from *, end k1.

Row 32 See row 4.

Rep rows 1–32.

mosaic maze

Colors A (dark) and B (light)

(multiple of 14 sts plus 2)

Note Sl sts wyib on RS rows, and sl sts wyif on WS rows.

Preparation row (WS) With A, purl.

Row 1 With B, k1, *k7, [sl 1, k1] 3 times, sl 1; rep from *, end k1.

Row 2 and all WS rows With same color as previous row, k1, p all sts worked and sl all sl-sts to last st, k1.

Row 3 With A, k1, *sl 1, k7, [sl 1, k1] 3 times; rep from *, end k1.

Row 5 With B, k2, *sl 1, k7, [sl 1, k1] 3 times; rep from * to end.

Row 7 With A, *[k1, sl 1] twice, k7, sl 1, k1, sl 1; rep from *, end k2.

Row 9 With B, k2, *sl 1, k1, sl 1, k7, [sl 1, k1] twice; rep from * to end.

Row 11 With A, *[k1, sl 1] 3 times, k7, sl 1; rep from *, end k2.

Row 13 With B, k1, *[k1, sl 1] 3 times, k7, sl 1; rep from *, end k1.

Row 15 With A, k1, *[sl 1, k1] 3 times, sl 1, k7; rep from *, end k1.

Row 17 With B, rep row 1.

Row 19 With A, *k7, [sl 1, k1] 3 times, sl 1; rep from *, end k2.

Row 21 With B, k6, *[sl 1, k1] 3 times, sl 1, k7; rep from *, end last rep k3.

Row 23 With A, k5, *[sl 1, k1] 3 times, sl 1, k7; rep from *, end last rep k4.

Row 25 With B, k4, *[sl 1, k1] 3 times, sl 1, k7; rep from *, end last rep k5.

Row 27 With A, k3, *[sl 1, k1] 3 times, sl 1, k7; rep from *, end last rep k6.

Row 29 With B, k2, *[sl 1, k1] 3 times, sl 1, k7; rep from * to end.

Row 31 With A, rep row 15.

Row 32 See row 2.

Rep rows 1–32.

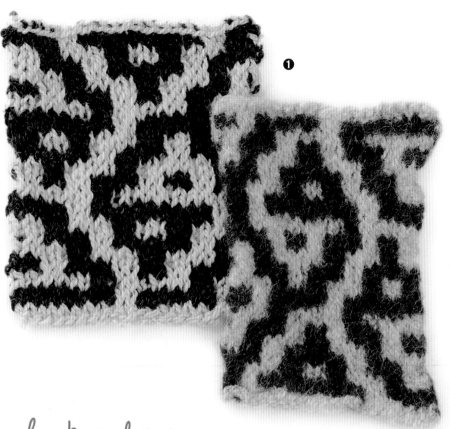

hook and eye

❶ Colors A (light) and B (dark) (multiple of 20 sts plus 2)

Note Sl sts wyib on RS rows, and sl sts wyif on WS rows.

Preparation row (WS) With A, purl.

Row 1 With B, k1, *k2, sl 2, k6, sl 2, k8; rep from *, end k1.

Row 2 and all WS rows With same color as previous row, k1, p all sts worked and sl all sl-sts to last st, k1.

Row 3 With A, k1, *k4, [sl 2, k6] twice; rep from *, end k1.

Row 5 With B, k1, *sl 2, k4, sl 2, k2; rep from *, end k1.

Row 7 With A, k1, *k2, [sl 2, k4] 3 times; rep from *, end k1.

Row 9 With B, k1, *k4, sl 2, k6, sl 2, k4, sl 2; rep from *, end k1.

Row 11 With A, k1, *sl 2, k4, sl 2, k2; rep from *, end k1.

Row 13 With B, k1, *k2, sl 2, k10, sl 2, k4; rep from *, end k1.

Row 15 With A, K1, *sl 2, k10, sl 2, k6; rep from *, end k1.

Row 17 With B, k1, *k4, sl 2, k2, sl 2; rep from *, end k1.

Row 19 With A, k1, *k2, sl 2, k6, sl 2, k4, sl 2, k2; rep from *, end k1.

Row 21 With B, k1, *[sl 2, k4] twice, sl 2, k6; rep from *, end k1.

Row 23 With A, k1, *k4, sl 2, k2, sl 2; rep from *, end k1.

Row 24 See row 2.

Rep rows 1–24.

chevron chic

❷ Colors A (light) and B (dark) (multiple of 24 sts plus 2)

Note Sl sts wyib on RS rows, and sl sts wyif on WS rows.

Preparation row (WS) With A, purl.

Row 1 With B, k1, *sl 1, k2; rep from *, end k1.

Row 2 and all WS rows With same color as previous row, k1, p all sts worked and sl all sl-sts to last st, k1.

Row 3 With A, k1, *k1, sl 1, [k2, sl 1] 3 times, k3, [sl 1, k2] 3 times, sl 1; rep from *, end k1.

Row 5 With B, k1, *k2, [sl 1, k2] 3 times, sl 1, k1, sl 1, [k2, sl 1] 3 times, k1; rep from *, end k1.

Row 7 With A, rep row 1.

Row 9 With B, rep row 3.

Row 11 With A, rep row 5.

Row 12 See row 2.

Rep rows 1–12.

lucky diamonds

❶ Colors A (light) and B (dark) (multiple of 16 sts plus 3)

Note Sl sts wyib on RS rows, and sl sts wyif on WS rows.

Preparation row (WS) With A, knit.

Row 1 With B, [k1, sl 1] 3 times, k7, *sl 1, [k1, sl 1] 4 times, k7; rep from *, end [sl 1, k1] 3 times.

Row 2 and all WS rows With same color as previous row, k all sts worked and sl all sl-sts.

Row 3 With A, k6, sl 1, [k1, sl 1] 3 times, *k9, sl 1, [k1, sl 1] 3 times; rep from *, end k6.

Row 5 With B, [k1, sl 1] twice, k5, sl 1, k5, *sl 1, [k1, sl 1] twice, k5, sl 1, k5; rep from *, end [sl 1, k1] twice.

Row 7 With A, k4, sl 1, k1, sl 1, *k5, sl 1, k1, sl 1; rep from *, end k4.

Row 9 With B, k1, sl 1, *k5, sl 1, [k1, sl 1] twice, k5, sl 1; rep from *, end k1.

Row 11 With A, k2, sl 1, k1, sl 1, k9, *sl 1, [k1, sl 1] 3 times, k9; rep from *, end last rep k2.

Row 13 With B, k5, sl 1, [k1, sl 1] 4 times, *k7, sl 1, [k1, sl 1] 4 times; rep from *, end k5.

Row 15 With A, k2, sl 1, k13, *sl 1, k1, sl 1, k13; rep from *, end sl 1, k2.

Row 17 Rep row 13.

Row 19 Rep row 11.

Row 21 Rep row 9.

Row 23 Rep row 7.

Row 25 Rep row 5.

Row 27 Rep row 3.

Row 28 See row 2.

Rep rows 1–28.

assyrian stripe

❷ Colors A (light) and B (dark) (multiple of 16 sts plus 1)

Note Sl sts wyib on RS rows, and sl sts wyif on WS rows.

Rows 1 and 2 With A, knit.

Row 3 (RS) With B, k1, *sl 1, k1; rep from * to end.

Row 4 and all WS rows through Row 26 With same color as previous row, k all sts worked and sl all sl-sts.

Row 5 With A, k8, *sl 1, k15; rep from *, end last rep k8.

Row 7 With B, k2, *[sl 1, k1] twice, sl 1, k3; rep from *, end last rep k2.

Row 9 With A, k7, *sl 3, k13; rep from *, end last rep k7.

Row 11 With B, k4, sl 1, k7; rep from *, end last rep k4.

Row 13 With A, k5, *sl 1, k1, sl 3, k1, sl 1, k9; rep from *, end last rep k5.

Rows 15, 17, 19, 21, 23 and 25 Rep rows 11, 9, 7, 5, 3 and 1.

Rows 27 and 28 With B, knit.

Row 29 With A, k1, *sl 1, k1; rep from * to end.

Row 30 and all rem WS rows through Row 50 Rep Row 4

Row 31 With B, k8, *sl 1, k15; rep from *, end last rep k8.

Row 33 With A, k2, *[sl 1, k1] twice, sl 1, k3; rep from *, end last rep k2.

Row 35 With B, k7, *sl 3, k13; rep from *, end last rep k7.

Row 37 With A, k4, sl 1, k7; rep from *, end last rep k4.

Row 39 With B, k5, *sl 1, k1, sl 3, k1, sl 1, k9; rep from *, end last rep k5.

Rows 41–51 Rep rows 37, 35, 33, 31, 29 and 27.

Row 52 With B, knit.

Rep rows 1–52.

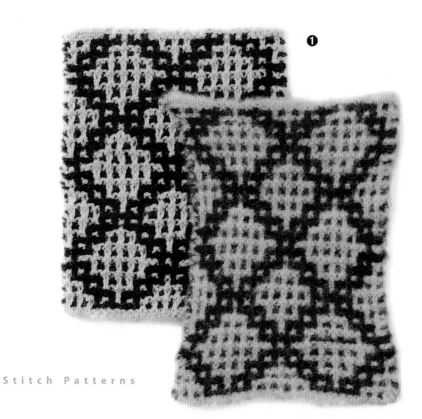

❶

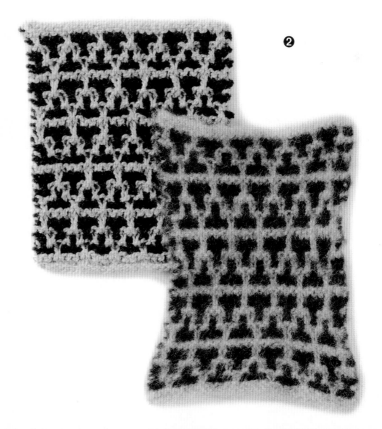

❷

color stitch patterns

Over the next several pages, you will see a wide variety of two- and three-color stitch patterns. They include lattice stitches and brick stitches that change dramatically when felted. These are slip-stitch patterns, in which you use only one color in each row, carrying the nonworking color or colors up the side of your work. When choosing color patterns for felting, try to achieve good color contrast and carefully consider the yarn weight you'll be using.

Yarn selection is very important with this group. Bold, bulky yarns will maintain the stitch quality and color pattern better than thinner yarns. Two-color patterns using thin yarns look very subtle after felting. Thicker yarns and bold contrast colors work best. Whatever yarns and patterns you choose, make a swatch and felt it before knitting your entire project.

trellis quilting

Colors A (light) and B (dark)

(multiple of 8 sts plus 1)

Preparation row (WS) With A, p1, *p1 wrapping yarn twice, p5, p1 wrapping yarn twice, p1; rep from * to end.

Row 1 With B, k1, *sl 1 wyib dropping extra wrap, k5, sl 1 wyib dropping extra wrap, k1; rep from * to end.

Row 2 With B, p1, *sl 1 wyif, p5, sl 1 wyif, p1; rep from * to end.

Row 3 With B, k1, *sl 1 wyib, k5, sl 1 wyib, k1; rep from * to end.

Row 4 With B, p to end dropping A sl-sts off needle to back.

Row 5 With A, k1, sl 1 wyib, k1, *k first dropped st, k1, k next dropped st, then [wyib sl last 3 sts back to LH needle, pass yarn to front, sl same 3 sts back to RH needle, pass yarn to back] twice, k1, sl 3 wyib, k1; rep from *, end last rep sl 1 wyib, k1.

Row 6 With A, p1, sl 1 wyif, *[p1, p1 wrapping yarn twice], p1, sl 3 wyif; rep from *, end last rep sl 1 wyif, p1.

Row 7 With B, k3, *sl 1 wyib dropping extra wrap, k1, sl 1 wyib dropping extra wrap, k5; rep from *, end last rep k3.

Row 8 With B, p3, *sl 1 wyif, p1, sl 1 wyif, p5; rep from *, end last rep p3.

Row 9 With B, k3, *sl 1 wyib, k1, sl 1 wyib, k5; rep from *, end last rep k3.

Row 10 With B, p to end dropping A sl-sts off needle to back.

Row 11 With A, k1, k first dropped st, k1, sl 3 wyib, k1; rep from * of row 5; end k last dropped st, k1.

Row 12 With A, p1, *p1 wrapping yarn twice, p1, sl 3 wyif, p1, p1 wrapping yarn twice, p1; rep from * to end.

Rep rows 1–12.

cool basket pattern

Colors A (light) and B (dark)
(multiple of 4 sts plus 1)

Row 1 (WS) With A, purl.

Row 2 With A, knit.

Row 3 With A, p4, *p1 wrapping yarn twice, p3; rep from *, end p1.

Row 4 With B, k4, *sl 1 wyib dropping extra wrap, k3; rep from *, end k1.

Rows 5 and 7 With B, k4, *sl 1 wyif, k3; rep from *, end k1.

Row 6 With B, k4, *sl 1 wyib, k3; rep from *, end k1.

Row 8 With A, k4, *drop sl-st off needle to front, k2, k dropped st, k1; rep from *, end k1.

Rows 9, 10 and 11 With A, rep rows 1, 2 and 3.

Rows 12, 13, 14 and 15 With B, rep rows 4, 5, 6 and 7.

Row 16 With A, k2, *sl 2 wyib, drop sl-st off needle to front, sl same 2 sts back to LH needle, k dropped st, k3; rep from *, end k3.

Rep rows 1–16.

cross-stitch stripe

Colors A (tan), B (green) and C (rust)
(multiple of 10 sts plus 1)

Cross 4 Drop next st off LH needle to front, k 3rd, first, and 2nd sts, then k dropped st.

Row 1 (WS) With A, purl.

Row 2 With A, knit.

Row 3 With A, p6, *p1 wrapping yarn twice, p2, p1 wrapping yarn twice, p6; rep from *, end last rep p1.

Row 4 With B, k1, *sl 1 dropping extra wrap, k2, sl 1 dropping extra wrap, k6; rep from * to end.

Row 5 With B, k6, *sl 1 wyif, k2, sl 1 wyif, k6; rep from *, end last rep k1.

Row 6 With B, k1, *sl 1 wyib, k2, sl 1 wyib, k6; rep from * to end.

Rows 7, 8 and 9 Rep rows 5, 6 and 5.

Row 10 With A, k1, *cross 4, k6; rep from * to end.

Row 11 With A, purl.

Row 12 With A, knit.

Row 13 With A, p1, *p1 wrapping yarn twice, p2, p1 wrapping yarn twice, p6; rep from * to end.

Row 14 With C, k6, *sl 1 dropping extra loop, k2, sl 1 dropping extra loop, k6; rep from *, end last rep k1.

Row 15 With C, k1, *sl 1 wyif, k2, sl 1 wyif, k6; rep from * to end.

Row 16 With C, k6, *sl 1 wyib, k2, sl 1 wyib, k6; rep from *, end last rep k1.

Rows 17, 18 and 19 Rep rows 15, 16 and 15.

Row 20 With A, k6, *cross 4, k6; rep from *, end last rep k1.

Rep rows 1–20.

royal quilting

Colors A (light) and B (dark)

(multiple of 6 sts plus 3)

Preparation row (RS) With A, knit.

Row 1 With A, k1, p1, *sl 5 wyib, p1; rep from *, end k1.

Row 2 With B, knit.

Row 3 With B, k1, p to last st, k1.

Row 4 With A, k1, sl 3 wyib, *k next st tog with row 1 strand; sl 5 wyib; rep from *, end last rep sl 3 wyib, k1.

Row 5 With A, k1, sl 3 wyib, *pl, sl 5 wyib; rep from *, end p1, sl 3 wyib, k1.

Rows 6 and 7 With B, rep rows 2 and 3.

Row 8 With A, k1, *k next st tog with row 5 strand, sl 5 wyib; rep from *, end k next st tog with row 5 strand, k1.

Rep rows 1–8.

surface quilting

Colors A (dark) and B (light)

(multiple of 10 sts plus 7)

Work strands With RH needle, pick up loops from 4 and 5 rows below and k tog with next st.

Cast on with A and purl 1 row.

Preparation row (RS) With B, k6, sl 5 wyif, *k5, sl 5 wyif; rep from *, end k6.

Row 1 With B, k6, sl 5 wyib, *k5, sl 5; rep from *, end k6.

Rows 2–5 With A, work in St st.

Row 6 With B, k1, sl 5 wyif, *k2, work strands, k2, sl 5 wyif; rep from *, end k1.

Row 7 With B, k1, sl 5 wyib, *k5, sl 5; rep from *, end k1.

Rows 8–11 Work in St st.

Row 12 With B, k3, work strands, *k2, sl 5 wyif, k2, work loops; rep from *, end k3.

Rep rows 1–12.

striped quilting

Colors A (light) and B (dark)

(multiple of 6 sts plus 2)

LPT Drop A sl-st to front, k2, k dropped st.

RPT Sl 2 wyib, drop A sl-st, sl same 2 sts back to LH needle, k dropped st, k2.

Row 1 (WS) With A, k1, *p1, k4, p1; rep from *, end k1.

Row 2 With B, k1, *sl 1 wyib, k4, sl 1 wyib; rep from *, end k1.

Row 3 With B, k1, *sl 1 wyif, k4, sl 1 wyif; rep from *, end k1.

Row 4 With A, k1, *LPT, RPT; rep from *, end k1.

Row 5 With A, k1, *k2, p2, k2; rep from *, end k1.

Row 6 With B, k1, *k2, sl 2 wyib, k2; rep from *, end k1.

Row 7 With B, k1, *k2, sl 2 wyif, k2; rep from *, end k1.

Row 8 With A, k1, *RPT, LPT; rep from *, end k1.

Rep rows 1–8.

Colors A (light) and B (dark)

(multiple of 6 sts plus 3)

Row 1 (RS) With A, knit.

Row 2 With A, purl.

Row 3 With B, k4, sl 1 wyib, *k5, sl 1 wyib; rep from *, end k4.

Row 4 With B, k4, sl 1 wyif, *k5, sl 1 wyif; rep from *, end k4.

Row 5 With B, p4, sl 1 wyib, *p5, sl 1 wyib; rep from *, end p4.

Row 6 Rep row 4.

Rows 7 With A, knit.

Rows 8 With A, purl.

Row 9 With B, k1, sl 1, *k5, sl 1; rep from *, end k1.

Row 10 With B, k1, sl 1 wyif, *k5, sl 1 wyif; rep from *, end k1.

Row 11 With B, p1, sl 1 wyib, *p5, sl 1 wyib; rep from *, end p1.

Row 12 Rep row 10.

Rep rows 1–12.

brick stitch bag

Flowers bloom on a brick background on this pretty bag, providing an interesting visual contrast between hard and soft textures.

MEASUREMENTS

Before felting

Approx 15"/38cm W x 20"/51.5cm L

After felting

Approx 12½"/32cm W x 14"/35.5cm L

MATERIALS

• 3 3½oz/100g balls (approx 110yd/101m) of Reynolds/JCA, Inc. **Lopi** (wool) in #53 brown (A)

• 1 ball each #9973 tan (B), #9983 green leaves (C) and #307 pink (D).

• Small amount dark purple for flower center (E)

• Size 13 (9mm) needles

• Tapestry needle

GAUGE

10½ sts and 18 1/2 rows = 4"/10cm in Brick st on size 13 (9mm) needles before felting.

BRICK PATTERN

(Multiple of 6 sts plus 3)

Row 1 (RS) With B, knit.

Row 2 With B, purl.

Row 3 With A, k4, sl 1 wyib, *k5, sl 1 wyib; rep from *, end k4.

Row 4 With A, k4, sl 1 wyif, *k5, sl 1 wyif; rep from *, end k4.

Row 5 With A, p4, sl 1 wyib, *p5, sl 1 wyib; rep from *, end p4.

Row 6 Rep row 4.

Row 7 With B, knit.

Row 8 With B, purl.

Row 9 With A, k1, sl 1 wyib, *k5, sl 1 wyib; rep from *, end k1.

Row 10 With A, k1, sl 1 wyif, *k5, sl 1 wyif; rep from *, end k1.

Row 11 With A, p1, sl 1 wyib, *p5, sl wl 1 wyib; rep from *, end p1.

Row 12 Rep row 10.

Rep rows 1–12.

BAG

Body

With B, cast on 39 sts and work in Brick pattern for 40"/101.5cm. Bind off.

Handle

With A, cast on 11 sts and work in St st for 65"/165cm. Bind off.

Leaves (make 8)

With C, cast on 3 sts.

Row 1 (WS) Purl.

Row 2 K in front and back of st, k to last st, k in front and back of st.

Rows 3–6 Rep rows 1 and 2.

Row 7 Purl.

Row 8 Ssk, k to last 2 sts, k2tog.

Rows 9–12 Rep rows 7 and 8.

Row 13 Purl.

Row 14 SK2P.

Fasten off.

Flowers (make 3)

With D, cast on 35 sts.

Row 1 (RS) *K1, bind off 5 sts (2 sts on RH needle); rep from * to end – 10 sts. Cut yarn and thread tail through rem sts on needle. Pull tightly and secure. With E, make a French knot (see Techniques) at center of flower.

FINISHING

Fold body of bag widthwise leaving a 10"/25.5cm flap. Sew side seams. Sew lengthwise seam of handle to form tube. Felt according to instructions on p. 8, placing handle, flowers and leaves in laundry bag. When all pieces have dried thoroughly, sew flowers and leaves to flap as pictured. Knot handle in 3 places as pictured and sew ends to inside side seams.

tip

Sometimes smaller pieces such as flowers and leaves don't get enough agitation in the washing machine. Put them through an extra wash cycle or do some hand-felting (see Chapter 5).

bold brick pattern

Colors A (dark) and B (light)

(multiple of 16 sts plus 7)

Row 1 (RS) With A, knit.

Row 2 With A, purl.

Row 3 With A, k2, sl 3 wyib, *k13, sl 3 wyib; rep from *, end k2.

Row 4 With B, k2, sl 3 wyif, *k13, sl 3 wyif; rep from *, end k2.

Row 5 With B, p2, sl 3 wyib, *p13, sl 3 wyib; rep from *, end p2.

Rows 6–10 Rep [rows 4 and 5] twice, then row 4.

Rows 11–14 With A, work in St st.

Row 15 With B, k10, sl 3 wyib, *k13, sl 3 wyib; rep from *, end k10.

Row 16 With B, k10, sl 3 wyif, *k13, sl 3 wyif; rep from *, end k10.

Row 17 With B, p10, sl 3 wyib, *p13, sl 3 wyib; rep from *, end p10.

Rows 18–22 [Rep rows 16 and 17] twice, then row 16.

Row 23 With A, knit.

Row 24 With A, purl.

Rep rows 1–24.

dashing stitch

Colors A (dark) and B (light)

(multiple of 6 sts plus 4)

Note Sl sts wyib on RS rows, and sl sts wyif on WS rows.

Row 1 (RS) With A, knit.

Row 2 With A, purl.

Rows 3 and 4 With B, k4, *sl 2, k4; rep from * to end.

Rows 5 and 6 With A, rep rows 1 and 2.

Rows 7 and 8 With B, k1, sl 2, *k4, sl 2; rep from *, end k1.

Rep rows 1–8.

box stitch

Colors A (light) and B (dark)
(multiple of 3 sts plus 3)

Row 1 (RS) With B, knit.

Row 2 With B, purl.

Row 3 With A, k1, sl 1 wyib, *k2, sl 1 wyib; rep from *, end k1.

Row 4 With A, k1, sl 1 wyif, *k2, sl 1 wyif; rep from *, end k1.

Rep rows 1–4.

sassy picot stripe

Colors A (dark) and B (light)

(multiple of 10 sts)

Row 1 (WS) With A, purl.

Row 2 With B, k2, *[k1, yo, k1, yo, k1, yo, k1] in next st, k9; rep from *, end last rep k6.

Row 3 With B, knit.

Row 4 With A, k1, *k2tog, k5, ssk, k7; rep from *, end last rep k6.

Row 5 With A, p6, *p2tog tbl, p1, sl 1 wyif, p1, p2tog, p7; rep from *, end last rep p1.

Row 6 With A, k1, *k2tog, sl 1 wyib, ssk, k7; rep from *, end last rep k6.

Row 7 With A, purl.

Row 8 With B, k7, *[k1, yo, k1, yo, k1, yo, k1] in next st, k9; rep from *, end last rep k2.

Row 9 With B, knit.

Row 10 With A, k6, *k2tog, k5, ssk, k7; rep from *, end last rep k1.

Row 11 With A, p1, *p2tog tbl, p1, sl 1 wyif, p1, p2tog, p7; rep from *, end last rep p6.

Row 12 With A, k6, *k2tog, sl 1 wyib, ssk, k7; rep from *, end last rep k1.

Rep rows 1–12.

shell dips 1

Colors A (light) and B (dark)
(multiple of 10 sts plus 2)

Preparation row (RS) With A, knit.

Row 1 With A, p8, *k1, p9; rep from *, end last rep p3.

Rows 2 and 4 With B, knit.

Rows 3 and 5 With B, purl.

Row 6 With A, *[k1, insert RH needle from front under next color A st 5 rows below and draw up a loop, k next st and pass loop over st] 3 times, k4; rep from *, end k2.

Row 7 With A, p3, *k1, p9; rep from *, end last rep p8.

Rows 8–11 With B, rep rows 2–5.

Row 12 With A, k5, *[k1, insert RH needle from front under next color A st 5 rows below and draw up a loop, k next st and pass loop over st] 3 times, k4; rep from *, end last rep k1.

Rep rows 1–12.

shell dips 2

Colors A (light) and B (dark)

(multiple of 14 sts plus 2)

Preparation row (WS) With A, knit.

Rows 1–6 With B, knit.

Row 7 With A, k9, *[working into st 5 rows below 3rd st on LH needle, insert RH needle into st from front and draw up a loop, k next st] 6 times in same st, k8; rep from *, end last rep k1.

Row 8 With A, k1, *[p2tog tbl] 3 times, p1, [p2tog] 3 times, k7; rep from *, end k1.

Rows 9–14 With B, knit.

Row 15 With A, k2, *[working into st 5 rows below 3rd st on LH needle, insert RH needle into st from front and draw up a loop, k next st] 6 times in same st, k8; rep from * to end.

Row 16 With A, k8, *[p2tog tbl] 3 times, p1, [p2tog] 3 times, k7; rep from *, end last rep k1.

Rep rows 1–16.

shadowbox

❶ Colors A (light), B (medium) and C (dark)

(multiple of 4 sts plus 3)

Row 1 (RS) With A, knit.

Row 2 With A, k1, *k1 wrapping yarn twice, k3; rep from *, end last rep k1.

Row 3 With B, k1, *sl 1 wyib dropping extra wrap, k3; rep from *, end last rep k1.

Row 4 With B, k1, *sl 1 wyif, k3; rep from *, end sl 1 wyif, k1.

Row 5 With C, k1, *sl 2 wyib, k2; rep from *, end sl 1 wyib, k1.

Row 6 With C, k1, sl 1 wyif, *p2, sl 2 wyif; rep f;rom *, end k1.

Rep rows 1–6.

two-tone lattice

❷ Colors A (light) and B (dark)

(multiple of 6 sts plus 2)

Preparation row (WS) With A, knit.

Row 1 With B, k1, sl 1 wyib, *k4, sl 2 wyib; rep from *, end k4, sl 1 wyib, k1.

Row 2 With B, p1, sl 1 wyif, *p4, sl 2 wyif; rep from *, end p4, sl 1 wyif, p1.

Row 3 With A, rep row 1.

Row 4 With A, k1, sl 1 wyif, *k4, sl 2 wyif; rep from *, end k4, sl 1 wyif, k1.

Row 5 With B, k3, *sl 2 wyib, k4; rep from *, end sl 2 wyib, k3.

Row 6 With B, p3, *sl 2 wyif, p4; rep from *, end sl 2 wyif, p3.

Row 7 With A, rep row 5.

Row 8 With A, k3, *sl 2 wyif, k4; rep from *, end sl 2 wyif, k3.

Rep rows 1–8.

house of cards

Colors A (light) and B (dark)

(multiple of 12 sts plus 3)

Note: On RS rows, sl sts wyib; on WS rows, sl sts wyif.

Row 1 (WS) With A, knit.

Row 2 With B, k1, *sl 1, k4, [sl 1, yo] twice, sl 1, k4; rep from *, end sl 1, k1.

Row 3 With B, k1, *sl 1, p4, sl 1, p1, sl 1, k1, sl 1, p4; rep from *, end sl 1, k1.

Row 4 With B, k1, *sl 1, k4, [sl 1, k1] twice, sl 1, k4; rep from *, end sl 1, k1.

Row 5 With B, k1, *sl 1, p4, [sl 1, p1] twice, sl 1, p4; rep from *, end sl 1, k1.

Row 6 With A, k5, *k2tog, k3, ssk, k7; rep from *, end last rep k5.

Row 7 With A, knit.

Row 8 With B, k1, *sl 1, k3, sl 1, yo, k1, sl 1, k1, yo, sl 1, k3; rep from *, end sl 1, k1.

Row 9 With B, k1, *sl 1, p3, [sl 1, p2] twice, sl 1, p3; rep from *, end sl 1, k1.

Row 10 With B, k1, *sl 1, k3, [sl 1, k2] twice, sl 1, k3; rep from *, end sl 1, k1.

Row 11 With B, rep row 9.

Row 12 With A, k4, *k2tog, k5, ssk, k5; rep from *, end last rep k4.

Row 13 With A, knit.

Row 14 With B, k1, *sl 1, k2, sl 1, yo, k2, sl 1, k2, yo, sl 1, k2; rep from *, end sl 1, k1.

Row 15 With B, k1, *sl 1, p2, [sl 1, p3] twice, sl 1, p2; rep from *, end sl 1, k1.

Row 16 With B, k1, *sl 1, k2, [sl 1, k3] twice, sl 1, k2; rep from *, end sl 1, k1.

Row 17 With B, rep row 15.

Row 18 With A, k3, *k2tog, k7, ssk, k3; rep from * to end.

Row 19 With A, knit.

Row 20 With B, k1, *sl 1, k1, sl 1, yo, k3, sl 1, k3, yo, sl 1, k1; rep from *, end sl 1, k1.

Row 21 With B, k1, *sl 1, p1, [sl 1, p4] twice, sl 1, p1; rep from *, end sl 1, k1.

Row 22 With B, k1, *sl 1, k1, [sl 1, k4] twice, sl 1, k1; rep from *, end sl 1, k1.

Row 23 With B, Rep row 21.

Row 24 With A, k2, *k2tog, k9, ssk, k1; rep from *, end k1.

Rep rows 1–24.

triple slip

❶ Colors A (dark) and B (light)

(multiple of 6 sts plus 5)

Row 1 (RS) With A, knit.

Row 2 With A, purl.

Row 3 With B, k1, sl 3 wyib, *sl 3 wyif, sl 3 wyib; rep from *,

end k1.

Row 4 With B, p1, sl 3 wyif, *sl 3 wyib, sl 3 wyif; rep from *,

end p1.

Rows 5 and 6 With A, rep rows 1 and 2.

Row 7 With B, k1, sl 3 wyif, *sl 3 wyib, sl 3 wyif; rep from *,

end k1.

Row 8 With B, p1, sl 3 wyib, *sl 3 wyif, sl 3 wyib; rep from *,

end p1.

Rep rows 1–8.

chimney tops

❷ Colors A (dark) and B (light)

(multiple of 4 sts plus 1)

Row 1 (RS) With A, knit.

Row 2 With A, purl.

Rows 3 and 4 With B, k1, *sl 3, k1; rep from * to end.

Row 5 With B, knit.

Row 6 With B, purl.

Row 7 With A, K3, sl 3, *k1, sl 3; rep from *, end k3.

Row 8 With A, p2, k1, *sl 3, k1; rep from *, end p2.

Rep rows 1–8.

shutter blocks

❶ Colors A (light) and B (dark)
(multiple of 10 sts plus 5)

Rows 1 and 3 (RS) With A, knit.

Rows 2 and 4 With A, purl.

woven plaid

❷ Colors A and B
(Multiple of 10 sts plus 2)

Note This pattern is worked back and forth on circular or double-pointed needles.

Preparation row (WS) With A, purl.

Row 1 (RS) With B, k1, *[sl 1 wyif, sl 1 wyib] twice, sl 1 wyif, k5; rep from *, end k1. Slide sts to other end of needle.

Row 2 With A, k1, *k5, sl 5 wyib; rep from *, end k1. Turn.

Row 3 With B, k1, *p5, [sl 1 wyif, sl 1 wyib] twice, sl 1 wyif; rep from *, end k1. Slide sts to

Rows 5 and 6 With B, knit.

Rows 7–10 With A, rep rows 1–4.

Row 11 With B, k1, sl 3 wyib, *k3, sl 1 wyib, k3, sl 3 wyib; rep from *, end k1.

other end of needle.

Row 4 With A, k1, *sl 5 wyif, p5; rep from *, end k1. Turn.

Rows 5–9 Rep rows 1–4, then row 1 once more.

Row 10 With A, k1 *k5, [sl 1 wyif, sl 1 wyib] twice, sl 1 wyif; rep from *, end k1. Turn.

Row 11 With B, k1, *p5, sl 5 wyif; rep from *, end k1. Slide sts to other end of needle.

Row 12 With A, k1, *[sl 1 wyif, sl 1 wyib] twice, sl 1 wyif, p5; rep from *, end k1. Turn.

Row 13 With B, k1, *sl 5 wyib, k5; rep from *, end k1. Slide sts to other end of needle.

Row 12 With B, k1, *sl 3 wyif, k3, sl 1 wyif, k3; rep from *, end sl 3 wyif, k1.

Row 13 With A, knit.

Row 14 With A, purl.

Rows 14–18 Rep rows 10-13, then row 10 once more.

Row 19 With B, k1, *p5, [sl 1 wyib, sl 1 wyif] twice, sl 1 wyib; rep from *, end k1. Slide sts to other end of needle.

Row 20 With A, k1, *sl 5 wyif, p5; rep from *, end k1. Turn.

Row 21 With B, k1, *[sl 1 wyib, sl 1 wyif] twice, sl 1 wyib, k5; rep from *, end k1. Slide sts to other end of needle.

Row 22 With A, k1, *k5, sl 5 wyib; rep from *, end k1. Turn.

Rows 23–27 Rep rows 19–22, then row 19

Rows 15–18 Rep rows 11–14.

Rows 19 and 20 Rep rows 11 and 12.

Rep rows 1–20.

once more.

Row 28 With A, k1, *[sl 1 wyib, sl 1 wyif] twice, sl 1 wyib, p5; rep from *, end k1. Turn.

Row 29 With B, k1, *sl 5 wyib, k5; rep from *, end k1. Slide sts to other end of needle.

Row 30 With A, k1, *k5, [sl 1 wyib, sl 1 wyif] twice, sl 1 wyib; rep from *, end k1. Turn.

Row 31 With B, k1, *p5, sl 5 wyif; rep from *, end k1. Slide sts to other end of needle.

Rows 32–35 Rep rows 28-31.

Row 36 Rep row 28.

Rep rows 1–36.

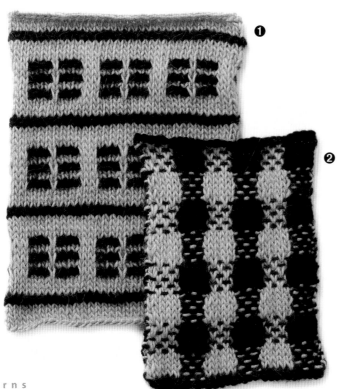

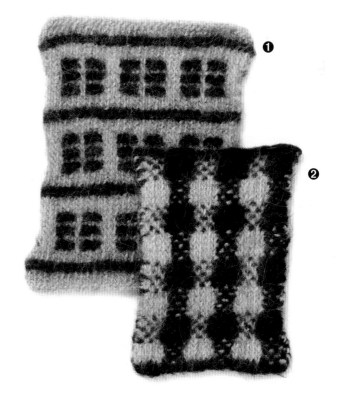

❶

❷

beaded stripe

❶ Colors A (dark) and B (light)

(multiple of 6 sts plus 5)

Row 1 (RS) With A, knit.

Row 2 With A, k1, *p3, k3; rep from *, end p3, k1.

Row 3 With B, k1, *sl 3 wyib, k3; rep from *, end sl 3 wyib, k1.

Row 4 With B, k1, p1, *sl 1 wyif, p5; rep from *, end sl 1 wyif, p1, k1.

Row 5 With B, knit.

Row 6 With B, k4, *p3, k3; rep from *, end k1.

Row 7 With A, k4, *sl 3 wyib, k3; rep from *, end k1.

Row 8 With A, k1, p4, *sl 1 wyif, p5; rep from *, end sl 1 wyif, p4, k1.

Rep rows 1–8.

string of purls

❷ Colors A (dark) and B (light)

(multiple of 12 sts)

Rows 1 and 3 (WS) With A, purl.

Row 2 With A, knit.

Row 4 With B, k11, *turn, sl 1 wyif, k3, turn, p4, k12; rep from *, end last rep k1.

Row 5 With B, k5, *turn, p4, turn, k3, sl 1 wyif, k12; rep from *, end last rep k7.

Row 6 With A, k8, *sl 2 wyib, k10; rep from *, end last rep k2.

Rows 7, 8 and 9 With A, rep rows 1, 2 and 3.

Row 10 With B, k5, *turn, sl 1 wyif, k3, turn, p4, k12; rep from *, end last rep k7.

Row 11 With B, k11, *turn, p4, turn, k3, sl 1 wyif, k12; rep from *, end last rep k1.

Row 12 With A, k2, *sl 2 wyib, k10; rep from *, end last rep k8.

Rep rows 1–12.

barred stripes

❸ Colors A (dark) and B (light)

(multiple of 4 sts plus 2)

Preparation row (WS) With A, purl.

Row 1 With B, k1, *sl 2 wyif, k2; rep from *, end k1.

Row 2 With B, k1, *p2, sl 2 wyif; rep from *, end k1.

Row 3 With A, k3, *sl 2 wyif, k2; rep from *, end sl 2 wyif, k1.

Row 4 With A, k1, *sl 2 wyif, p2; rep from *, end k1.

Rep rows 1–4.

wave and box

❶ Colors A (light) and B (dark)
(multiple of 10 sts plus 5)

Note This pattern is worked back and forth on circular or double-pointed needles.

Row 1 (WS) With A, purl.

Row 2 With B, knit. Slide sts to other end of needle.

Row 3 With A, knit.

Row 4 With B, p1, *sl 3 wyif, p7; rep from *, end sl 3 wyif, p1. Slide sts to other end of needle.

Row 5 With A, purl.

Row 6 With B, k1, *sl 3 wyib, k7; rep from *, end sl 3 wyib, k1. Slide sts to other end of needle.

Row 7 With A, knit.

Row 8 With B, rep row 4. Slide sts to other end of needle.

Rows 9, 10 and 11 Rep rows 1, 2 and 3.

Row 12 With B, p6, *sl 3 wyif, p7; rep from *, end sl 3 wyif, p6. Slide sts to other end of needle.

Row 13 With A, purl.

Row 14 With B, k6, *sl 3 wyib, k7; rep from *, end sl 3 wyib, k6. Slide sts to other end of needle.

Row 15 With A, knit.

Row 16 With B, rep row 12. Slide sts to other end of needle.

Rep rows 1–16.

diamond argyle

❷ Colors A (light) and B (dark)

(multiple of 14 sts plus 7)

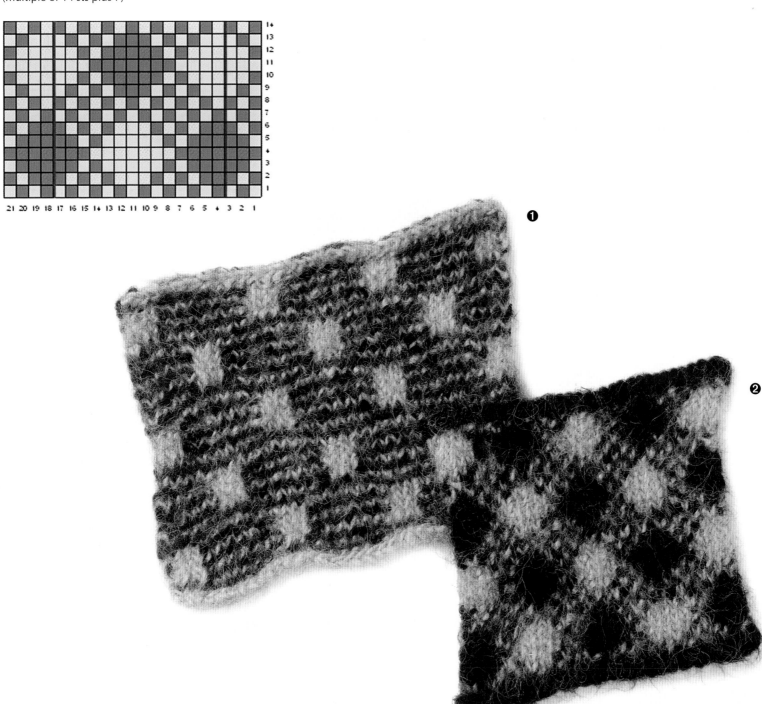

dice check

❶ Colors A (dark), B (tan) and C (rust)
(multiple of 4 sts plus 2)
Row 1 (WS) With A and purl.

Row 2 With B, k1, sl 1 wyib, *k2, sl 2 wyib; rep from *,
end k2, sl 1 wyib, k1.
Row 3 With B, p1, sl 1 wyif, *p2, sl 2 wyif; rep from *,
end p2, sl 1 wyif, p1.

Row 4 With A, knit.
Row 5 With C, p2, *sl 2 wyif, p2; rep from * to end.
Row 6 With C, k2, *sl 2 wyib, k2; rep from * to end.
Rep rows 1–6.

tiny check

❷ Colors A (light) and B (dark)
(multiple of 2 plus 1)
Note This pattern is worked back and forth on
circular or double-pointed needles.

Row 1 (WS) With A, purl.
Row 2 (RS) With B, k1, *sl 1 wyib, k1; rep from * to
end. Slide sts to other end of needle.
Row 3 (RS) With A, knit.

Row 4 (WS) With B, p2, *sl 1 wyif, p1; rep from *, end
p1. Slide sts to other end of needle.
Rep rows 1–4.

slip stitch stripes

❸ Colors A (light) and B (dark)
(multiple of 2 plus 1)
Preparation row (WS) With A, purl.

Rows 1 and 3 With B, k1, *sl 1 wyib, k1; rep from * to end.

Row 2 With B, p1, *sl 1 wyif, p1; rep from * to end.

Row 4 With B, purl.

Rows 5–8 With A, rep rows 1–4.

Rep rows 1–8.

swiss check

❹ Colors A (light) and B (dark)
(multiple of 4 sts plus 1)

Row 1 (WS) With A, purl.

Row 2 With B, k1, sl 1 wyib, *k1, sl 3 wyib; rep from *, end k1, sl 1, k1.

Row 3 With B, k1, *p3, sl 1 wyif; rep from *, end p3, k1.

Row 4 With A, k2, *sl 1 wyib, k3; rep from *, end sl 1, k2.

Row 5 With A, purl.

Row 6 With B, k1, *sl 3 wyib, k1; rep from * to end.

Row 7 With B, k1, p1, *sl 1 wyif, p3; rep from *, end sl 1, p1, k1.

Row 8 With A, k4, *sl 1 wyib, k3; rep from *, end k1.

Rep rows 1–8.

broken plaid

❶ Colors A (light), B (background) and C (dark)
(multiple of 8 sts plus 7)
Row 1 (RS) With A, knit.
Row 2 With A, k3, k1 wrapping yarn 3 times, *k7, k1 wrapping yarn 3 times; rep from *, end k3.
Row 3 With B, k3, *sl 1 wyib dropping extra wraps, k3; rep from * to end.

Row 4 With B, p3, *sl 1 wyif, p3; rep from * to end.
Row 5 With C, k3, *sl 1 wyib, k7; rep from *, end sl 1 wyib, k3.
Row 6 With C, k3, *sl 1 wyif, k7; rep from *, end sl 1 wyif, k3.
Rows 7 and 8 With B, rep rows 3 and 4.
Row 9 With C, knit.

Row 10 With C, k7, *k1 wrapping yarn 3 times, k7; rep from * to end.
Rows 11 and 12 With B, rep rows 3 and 4.
Row 13 With A, k7, *sl 1 wyib, k7; rep from * to end.
Row 14 With A, k7, *sl 1 wyif, k7; rep from * to end.
Rows 15 and 16 With B, rep rows 3 and 4.
Rep rows 1–16.

bean sprouts

❷ Colors A (dark) and B (light)
(multiple of 6 sts plus 5)
Row 1 (RS) With A, knit.
Row 2 With A, purl.
Row 3 With B, k2, *sl 1 wyib, k1; rep from *, end k1.
Row 4 With B, k1, *[k1, sl 1 wyif] twice, p1, sl 1 wyif;

rep from *, end k1, sl 1 wyif, k2.
Rows 5 and 7 With A, k5, *sl 1 wyib, k5; rep from * to end.
Rows 6 and 8 With A, p5, *sl 1 wyif, p5; rep from * to end.
Rows 9 and 10 With A, rep rows 1 and 2.
Row 11 With B, k1, *sl 1wyib, k1; rep from * to end.

Row 12 With B, k1, *sl 1 wyif, p1, [sl 1 wyif, k1] twice; rep from *, end sl 1 wyif, p1, sl 1 wyif, k1.
Rows 13 and 15 With A, k2, *sl 1 wyib, k5; rep from *, end sl 1 wyib, k2.
Rows 14 and 16 With A, p2, *sl 1 wyif, p5; rep from *, end sl 1 wyif, p2.
Rep rows 1–16.

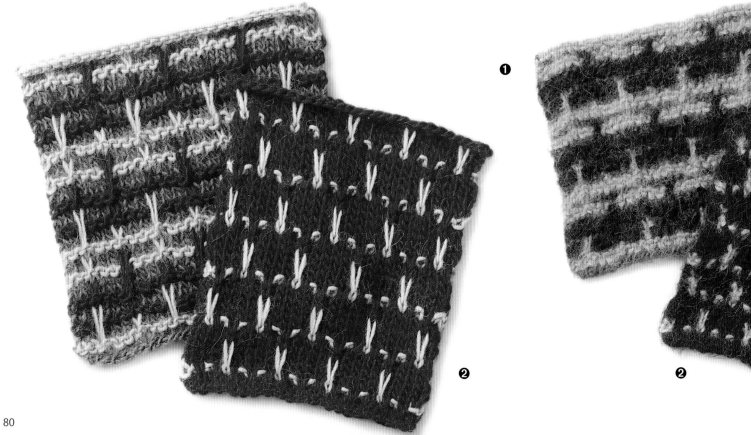

❶

❷

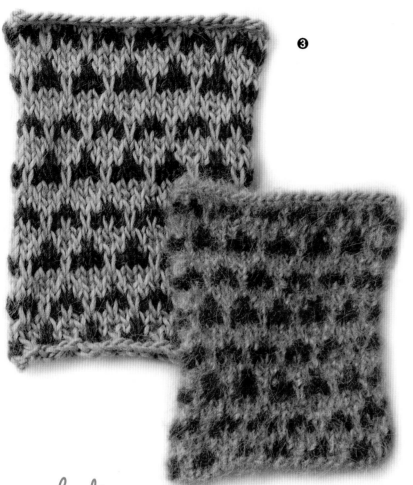

buds

❸ Colors A (medium), B (dark) and C (light)
(multiple of 4 sts plus 1)
Note On RS rows sl sts wyib, on WS rows sl sts wyif.
Row 1 (WS) With A, purl.
Row 2 With B, k2, *sl 1, k3; rep from *, end last rep k2.
Row 3 With B, p2, *sl 1, p3; rep from *, end last rep p2.
Row 4 With C, k4, *sl 1, k3; rep from *, end k1.
Row 5 With C, p4, *sl 1, p3; rep from *, end p1.
Row 6 With A, k1, *sl 1, k1; rep from * to end.
Row 7 With A, purl.
Row 8 With B, k2, *sl 1, k1; rep from *, end k1.
Row 9 With B, p4, *sl 1, k1; rep from *, end p1.
Row 10 With C, k2, *sl 1, k3; rep from *, end last rep k2.
Row 11 With C, purl.
Row 12 With A, k1, *sl 1, k1; rep from * to end.
Rep rows 1–12.

ribbon bows

❹ Colors A (light) and B (dark)
(multiple of 4 sts plus 3)
Preparation row (WS) With A, purl.
Row 1 With B, k1, *sl 1 wyib, k3; rep from *, end last rep k1.
Row 2 With B, k1, *sl 1 wyif, k1, k1 wrapping yarn 3 times, k1; rep from *, end sl 1 wyif, k1.
Row 3 With A, k3, *sl 1 wyib dropping extra wraps, k3; rep from * to end.
Row 4 With A, p3, *sl 1 wyib, p3; rep from * to end.
Row 5 With A, k3, *sl 1 wyib, k3; rep from * to end.
Rows 6, 7 and 8 With A, rep rows 4 and 5, then row 4.
Rep rows 1–8.

mandarin tile

❶ Colors A (background), B (rust) and C (tan)
(multiple of 8 sts plus 6)

Note On RS rows sl sts wyib, on WS rows sl sts wyif.

Preparation row (WS) With C, purl.

Row 1 With A, knit.

Rows 2, 3 and 4 With A, k6, *sl 2, k6; rep from * to end.

Row 5 With B, k6, *sl 2, k6; rep from * to end.

Row 6 With B, *p6, sl 2; rep from *, end p6.

Rows 7 and 8 With B, rep rows 5 and 6.

Row 9 With A, knit.

Rows 10, 11 and 12 With A, k2, sl 2, *k6, sl 2; rep
from *, end k2.

Row 13 With C, k2, sl 2, *k6, sl 2; rep from *, end k2.

Row 14 With C, p2, sl 2, *p6, sl 2; rep from *, end p2.

Rows 15 and 16 Rep rows 13 and 14.

Rep rows 1–16.

florentine frieze

❷ Colors A (light) and B (dark)
(multiple of 4 sts plus 1)

Row 1 (WS) With A, purl.

Row 2 With B, k1, *sl 1 wyib, sl 1 wyif, sl 1 wyib, k1;
rep from * to end.

Row 3 With B, p1, *sl 3 wyib, yo, p1; rep from * to end.

Row 4 With A, knit dropping all yo's.

Row 5 With A, purl.

Row 6 With B, k1, *sl 1 wyib, pick up loose B strand
and k next st catching strand behind st, sl 1 wyib, k1;
rep from * to end.

Row 7 With B, k1, *sl 1 wyif, p1, sl 1 wyif, k1; rep from

* to end.

Row 8 With A, knit.

Row 9 With A, purl.

Row 10 With B, k1, *sl 1 wyif, k1; rep from * to end.

Rows 11–20 Rep rows 1–10 reversing colors.

Rep rows 1–20.

vertical chain links

❸ Colors A (light) and B (dark)

(multiple of 8 sts plus 2)

Note On RS rows sl sts wyib, on WS rows sl sts wyif.

Preparation row (WS) With A, purl.

Row 1 With B, k3, *sl 1, k2, sl 1, k4; rep from *, end last rep k3.

Row 2 With B, p3, *p4, sl 1, p2, sl 1; rep from *, end p3.

Row 3 With A, k1, sl 1, *k2, sl 2; rep from *, end k2, sl 1, k1.

Row 4 With A, p1, sl 1, p2, *sl 2, p2; rep from *, end sl 1, p1.

Rows 5 and 6 With B, rep rows 1 and 2.

Row 7 With A, k2, *sl 1, k4, sl 1, k2; rep from * to end.

Row 8 With A, *p2, sl 1, p4, sl 1; rep from *, end p2.

Rows 9 and 10 With B, rep rows 3 and 4.

Rows 11 and 12 With A, rep rows 7 and 8.

Rep rows 1–12.

scot tile

❹ Colors A (background), B (light), C (medium) and D (dark)

(multiple of 10 sts plus 4)

Note On RS rows sl sts wyib, on WS rows sl sts wyif.

Row 1 (RS) With A, knit.

Row 2 With A, purl.

Row 3 With B, k1, *sl 2, k8; rep from *, end sl 2, k1.

Row 4 With C, p1, sl 3, *p6, sl 4; rep from *, end p6, sl 3, p1.

Row 5 With C, k1, sl 3, *k6, sl 4; rep from *, end k6, sl 3, k1.

Row 6 With B, p1, *sl 2, p8; rep from *, end sl 2, p1.

Rows 7 and 8 With A, rep rows 1 and 2.

Row 9 With B, k6, *sl 2, k8; rep from *, end sl 2, k6.

Row 10 With D, p5, *sl 4, p6; rep from *, end sl 4, p5.

Row 11 With D, k5, *sl 4, k6; rep from *, end sl 4, k5.

Row 12 With B, p6, *sl 2, p8; rep from *, end sl 2, p6.

Rep rows 1–12.

❸

❹

lattice lass

Colors A (light) and B (dark)

(multiple of 6 sts plus 2)

Preparation row (WS) With A, knit.

Row 1 With B, k1, sl 1 wyib, *k4, sl 2 wyib; rep from *, end k4, sl 1, k1.

Row 2 With B, p1, sl 1 wyif, *p4, sl 2 wyif; rep from *, end p4, sl 1, p1.

Row 3 With A, rep row 1.

Row 4 With A, k1, sl 1 wyif, *k4, sl 2 wyif; rep from *, end k4, sl 1, k1.

Row 5 With B, k3, *sl 2 wyib, k4; rep from *, end sl 2, k3.

Row 6 With B, p3, *sl 2 wyif, p4; rep from *, end sl 2, p3.

Row 7 With A, rep row 5.

Row 8 With A, k3, *sl 2 wyif, k4; rep from *, end sl 2, k3.

Rep rows 1–8.

one-color slip-stitch patterns

On this page I've shown you two interesting one-color slip-stitch patterns that produce a beautiful texture after felting.

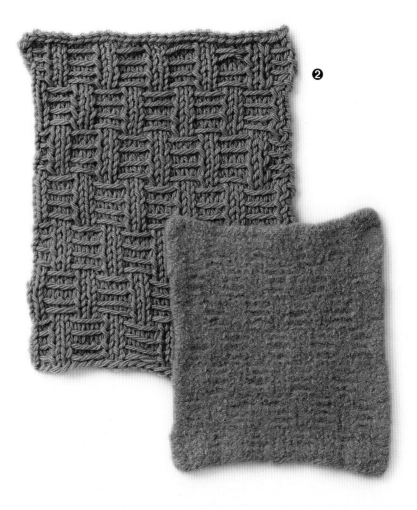

slipped zigzag

❶ (multiple of 5 sts plus 2)

Row 1 and all WS rows Purl.

Row 2 Knit.

Rows 4 and 6 P2, *sl 3 wyif, p2; rep from * to end.

Rep rows 1–6.

basketweave slip stitch

❷ (multiple of 6 sts plus 2)

Row 1 and all WS rows Purl.

Rows 2, 4, 6 and 8 K1, sl 2 wyif, k2, *sl 4 wyif, k2; rep from *, end sl 2 wyif, k1.

Rows 10, 12, 14 and 16 K2, *sl 4 wyif, k2; rep from * to end.

Rep rows 1–16.

lace: the hole truth

Lace stitches are tricky, but they can be felted successfully. When felting knitted lace, your goal is to keep the yarn overs that form the holes from shrinking together and closing up the lovely patterns you have knit.

Use a needle three sizes larger than the suggested one. After your piece is knitted, block it out. Shetland wool works best with lace and embroidery because it takes longer to felt, giving you more time to control the

process. Here I've chosen a wide range of lace techniques, including mesh stitches, grand eyelets, chevrons, waves and trellis laces.

ribbon rib

dainty chevron

snowflake

starlight

checkmate mesh

lace leaf

Knitting lace is an intricate process, so it is certainly worth doing a test swatch to avoid felting problems. If you are felting a large garment, make sure all the openings are secured before felting. For example, if you are making a lace vest, sew the pieces of the vest together and baste the armholes and the fronts together with cotton thread, then remove the thread after felting. This will keep the armholes from ruffling. You may also want to sew cotton thread around the outer neck edge. Basting is not necessary for edges knitted in ribbing.

Stitch patterns are on p. 88.

ribbon rib

dainty chevron

snowflake

starlight

checkmate mesh

lace leaf

starlight

(multiple of 6 sts plus 5)

S2KP Sl 2 sts knitwise, k1, p2sso.

SK2P Sl 1 st, k2tog, psso.

Row 1 and all WS rows Purl.

Row 2 K2, *yo, ssk, k1, yo ssk, k1 tbl; rep from *, end yo, ssk, k1.

Row 4 K3, *k2tog, yo, k1 tbl, yo, ssk, k1 tbl; rep from *, end k2.

Row 6 K2, k2tog, *yo, S2KP, yo, SK2P; rep from *, end yo, S2KP, yo, ssk, k2.

Row 8 K3, *k1 tbl, yo, k1, yo, k1 tbl, k1; rep from *, end k2.

Row 10 K2, *yo, ssk, k1 tbl, yo, ssk, k1; rep from *, end yo, ssk, k1.

Row 12 *K2tog, yo, k1 tbl, yo, ssk, k1 tbl; rep from *, end k2tog, yo, k1 tbl, yo, ssk.

Row 14 K1, *yo, S2KP, yo, SK2P; rep from *, end yo, S2KP, yo, k1.

Row 16 K1, k1 tbl, *k1, yo, k1 tbl, k1, k1 tbl, yo; rep from *, end k1, k1 tbl, k1.

Rep rows 1–16.

ribbon rib

(multiple of 14 sts plus 1)

Row 1 and all WS rows Purl.

Rows 2, 4, 6, 8 and 10 K1, *yo, k3, SK2P, yo, k1, yo, k3tog, k3, yo, k1; rep from * to end.

Rows 12, 14, 16, 18 and 20 K1, *yo, k3tog, k3, yo, k1, yo, k3, SK2P, yo ,k1; rep from * to end.

Rep rows 1–20.

dainty chevron

(multiple of 8 sts plus 1)

S2KP Sl 2 sts knitwise, k1, p2sso.

S2PP Sl 2 sts as if to p2tog, p1, p2sso.

Row 1 (RS) K1, *ssk, [k1, yo] twice, k1, k2tog, k1; rep from * to end.

Row 2 P1, *p2tog, [p1, yo] twice, p1, p2tog tbl, p1; rep from * to end.

Row 3 K1, *yo, ssk, k3, k2tog, yo, k1; rep from * to end.

Row 4 P2, *yo, p2tog, p1, p2tog tbl, yo, p3; rep from *, end last rep p2.

Row 5 K3, *yo, S2KP, yo, k5; rep from *, end last rep k3.

Row 6 Rep row 2.

Row 7 Rep row 1.

Row 8 P1, *yo, p2tog, p3, p2tog tbl, yo, p1; rep from * to end.

Row 9 K2, *yo, ssk, k1, k2tog, yo, k3; rep from *, end last rep k2.

Row 10 P3, *yo, S2PP, yo, p5; rep from *, end last rep p3.

snowflake

(multiple of 8 sts plus 5)

Row 1 and all WS rows Purl.

Row 2 K4, *ssk, yo, k1, yo, k2tog, k3; rep from *, end k1.

Row 4 K5, *yo, S2KP, yo, k5; rep from * to end.

Row 6 Rep row 2.

Row 8 Ssk, yo, k1, yo, k2tog, *k3, ssk, yo, k1, yo, k2tog; rep from * to end.

Row 10 K1, *yo, S2KP, yo, k5; rep from *, end last rep k1.

Row 12 Rep row 8.

Rep rows 1–12.

checkmate mesh

(multiple of 10 sts plus 4)

Row 1 and all WS rows Purl.

Row 2 K4, *yo, ssk, k1, [k2tog, yo] twice, k3; rep from * to end.

Row 4 *K3, [yo, ssk] twice, k1, k2tog, yo; rep from *, end k4.

Row 6 K2, *[yo, ssk] 3 times, k4; rep from *, end yo, ssk.

Row 8 K1, *[yo, ssk] 4 times, k2; rep from *, end yo, ssk, k1.

Rows 10, 12 and 14 Rep rows 6, 4 and 2.

Row 16 K2tog, yo, *k4, [k2tog, yo] 3 times; rep from *, end k2.

Row 18 K1, k2tog, yo, *k2, [k2tog, yo] 4 times; rep from *, end k1.

Row 20 Rep row 16.

Rep rows 1–20.

lace leaf

(multiple of 9 sts plus 3)

Row 1 (RS) Knit.

Row 2 Purl.

Row 3 K3, *k2tog, k1, yo, k6; rep from * to end.

Row 4 P1, *p6, yo, p1, p2tog; rep from *, end p2.

Row 5 K1, *k2tog, k1, yo, k6; rep from *, end k2.

Row 6 P3, *p6, yo, p1, p2tog; rep from * to end.

Rows 7 and 8 Rep rows 1 and 2.

Row 9 *K6, yo, k1, ssk; rep from *, end k3.

Row 10 P2, *p2tog tbl, p1, yo, p6; rep from *, end p1.

Row 11 K2, *k6, yo, k1, ssk; rep from *, end k1.

Row 12 *P2tog tbl, p1, yo, p6; rep from *, end p3.

Rep rows 1–12.

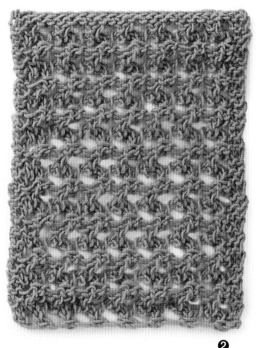

crown eyelet

❶ (multiple of 5 sts)

Rows 1–4 Knit.

Row 5 K1, *k1 wrapping yarn 3 times; rep from * to end.

Row 6 *Sl 5 dropping extra wraps, sl these 5 sts back to LH needle and work as foll: k1, [p1, k1] twice; rep from * to end.

Rows 7 and 8 Knit.

Rep rows 1–8.

cat's eye

❷ (multiple of 4 sts)

Row 1 (RS) K4, *[yo] twice, k4; rep from * to end.

Row 2 P2, *p2tog, [p1, k1] into double yo, p2tog; rep from *, end p2.

Row 3 K2, yo, *k4, [yo] twice; rep from *, end k4, yo, k2.

Row 4 P3, *[p2tog] twice, [p1, k1] into double yo; rep from *, end [p2tog] twice, p3.

Rep rows 1–4.

cane stitch

❶ (multiple of 3 sts plus 4)

Row 1 K2, *SK2P, [yo] twice; rep from *, end k2.

Row 2 K2, *[p1, k1] into double yo, p1; rep from *, end k2.

Row 3 Knit.

Rep rows 1–3.

grand eyelet

❷ (multiple of 8 sts)

RT K2tog but do not slip from needle; insert RH needle between the sts just knitted tog and k the first st again, then sl both sts from needle tog.

Row 1 (WS) Purl.

Row 2 *[K2tog] twice, [yo] twice, [ssk] twice; rep from * to end.

Row 3 *P2tog tbl, [p1, k1] 3 times into double yo, p2tog; rep from * to end.

Row 4 K1, *k6, RT; rep from *, end k7.

Row 5 Purl.

Row 6 K4, *[k2tog] twice, [yo] twice, [ssk] twice; rep from *, end k4.

Row 7 P4, *p2tog tbl, [p1, k1] 3 times into double yo, p2tog; rep from *, end p4.

Row 8 K3, *RT, k6; rep from *, end k3.

Rep rows 1–8.

tip

I used a nonplied wool yarn for these swatches, and it felted too quickly. A plied yarn with a tight twist might have worked better.

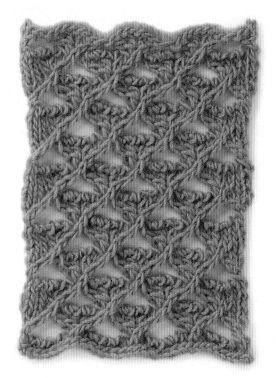

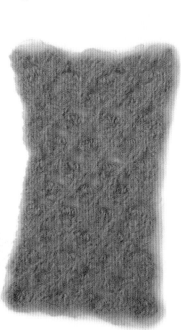

❶

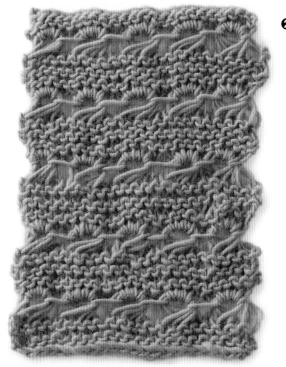

❷

4
a variety of techniques

This chapter samples a wide range of felting possibilities. I'll show you how to use intarsia and other colorwork techniques, duplicate stitch and other types of embroidery, yarn combinations, entrelac and woven drop-stitch patterns in felted projects. All of these can make striking knit pieces such as hats, bags and sweaters. Included are special tips for each of them.

intarsia

Intarsia patterns have blocks of colorwork and are knitted from charts. Normally, you would weave in all the yarn ends after you finish knitting, but if you have the nerve, you can leave the yarn ends loose before felting and cut the ends off after the piece is felted. The felting process will secure the yarn ends in place—good news for people who don't like weaving in ends. Leave the ends no more than 2½ inches (6 cm) long if you're going to cut them after felting. If they are longer, they may tangle during felting. I suggest knitting and felting a swatch with the yarn you've chosen for your project to make sure the felting process secures the ends. Again, different yarns felt differently.

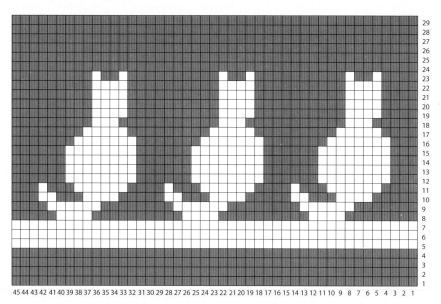

Color Key

■ A

□ B

moonlit cats

stranded colorwork techniques

Because of the two-color stranding method used for Fair Isle and Argyle patterns, the knitted piece is dense. As a result, it shrinks less when felted than pieces produced using other techniques. Keep this in mind when designing a colorwork or Fair Isle piece that you intend to felt.

The swatches on this and the following pages show classic colorwork patterns. Although some of them look very complicated, each row includes only two colors. Notice how felting makes the design look richer and more subtle.

linear check

❶ Colors A, B, C and D (multiple of 4 sts plus 2)

wallpaper stripe

❷ Colors A and B (multiple of 6 sts)

fleur-de-lis plaid

❶ Colors A and B

(multiple of 12 sts plus 1)

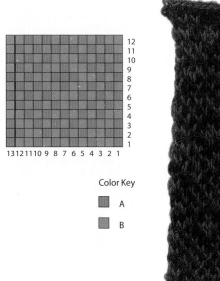

Color Key

A

B

❶

three-color argyle

❷ Colors A, B and C

(multiple of 19 sts)

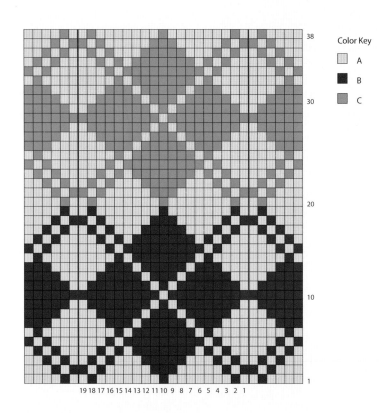

Color Key

A

B

C

❷

shield of argyle

❶

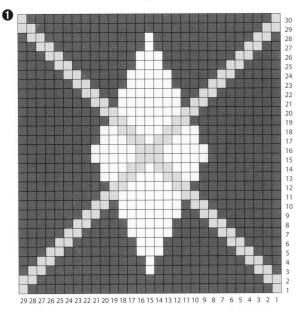

Color Key	
■	A
□	B
▨	C

pinstripe

❷ Colors A (light) and B (dark)

(multiple of 2 sts)

Cast on with A.

Preparation row (WS) With A, knit.

Row 1 With B, k1, *k1, sl 1 wyib; rep from *, end k1.

Row 2 With B, p1, *sl 1 wyif, p1; rep from *, end p1.

Row 3 With A, k1, *sl 1 wyib, k1 tbl; rep from *, end k1.

Row 4 With A, p1, *p1, sl 1 wyif; rep from *, end p1.

Rep rows 1–4.

tip

When knitting a piece you intend to felt, remember that light and dark colors may felt differently. Your test swatch will be invaluable in this situation!

❷ **❷**

❶ **❶**

fair isle hat

This Fair Isle hat is knitted in the round and shaped using quilt batting before felting.

FINISHED MEASUREMENTS

Before felting

Approx 25"/63.5cm circumference x 12"/30.5cm H

After felting

Approx 20"/51cm circumference x 8"/20.5cm H

MATERIALS

1 3½oz/100g ball (each approx 200yd/180m) of Harrisville **New England Highland** (wool) in #24 periwinkle (A)

1 ball each in #22 plum (B), #27 cornflower (C), #21 violet (D), #18 aubergine (E)

Size 9 (5.5mm) circular needle and set of dpns

2 layers of 26"/66cm x 14"/35.5cm quilt batting

Sewing needle and thread

Tapestry needle

GAUGE

20 sts and 20 rows = 4"/10cm in St st over St st Fair Isle pattern.

HAT

With A, cast on 114 sts. Pm and join for working in the round. K 2 rnds.

Inc rnd K6, *m1, k7, m1, k5; rep from * —132 sts.

Work in St st for 3"/7.5cm, then work 49 rows of Chart.

CROWN

Rnd 1 With E, *k2tog; rep from * around—60 sts.

Remove marker. Cont to k2tog around until 4 sts rem. Work in i-cord (see Techniques) for 5½"/14cm. Slip 2nd, 3rd and 4th sts over first st. Fasten off.

FINISHING

Roll batting into a 3¼"/8.5cm diameter cylinder and stitch in place with needle and thread. Bring ends together to form a ring and sew securely. Roll brim to inside of hat, inserting batting. With A, sew cast-on edge to dec rnd, easing edge in place to enclose batting and shape brim. Brim should fit loosely around batting to allow for shrinkage. Felt according to instructions on p. 8. Stitch end of I-cord to base to form loop.

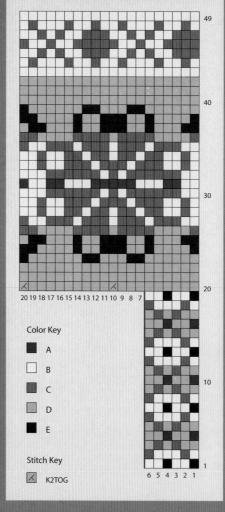

Color Key

- A
- B
- C
- D
- E

Stitch Key

- K2TOG

tip

Make sure your knit piece fits loosely around the quilt batting so it has room to shrink. Otherwise you will have a shibori brim.

fancy fair isle

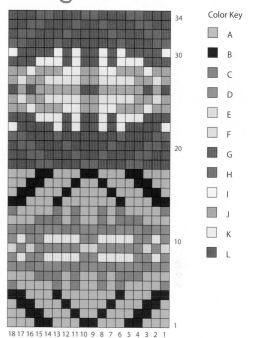

Color Key	
	A
	B
	C
	D
	E
	F
	G
	H
	I
	J
	K
	L

from my readers

When felting a knitted item that has multiple colors, I add a cup of vinegar to the hot water. This prevents the colors from running into each other.

—J. Isobel Cooper Marks

colorblocks

Colorwork patterns like this one felt beautifully. This colorblocking technique is associated with the artist and designer Horst Schulz. It's a great way to use yarn leftovers as well as create unique felted projects.

patchwork squares

Colors A and B (various)

COLUMN 1

Square 1

With A, cast on 23 sts.

Row 1 (WS) With A, k10, k3tog, k10.

Row 2 With B, knit.

Row 3 With B, p9, p3tog, p9.

Row 4 With A, knit.

Row 5 With A, k8, k3tog, k8.

Row 6 With B, knit.

Row 7 With B, p7, p3tog, p7.

Row 8 With A, knit.

Row 9 With A, k6, k3tog, k6.

Row 10 With B, knit.

Row 11 With B, p5, p3tog, p5.

Row 12 With A, knit.

Row 13 With A, k4, k3tog, k4.

Row 14 With B, knit.

Row 15 With B, p3, p3tog, p3.

Row 16 With A, knit.

Row 17 With A, k2, k3tog, k2.

Row 18 With B, knit.

Row 19 With B, k1, k3tog, k1.

Row 20 With A, knit.

Row 21 P3tog, do not cut yarn. *With RS facing, pick up and k 11 sts across top of square 1, cast on 11 sts. Rep rows 1–21. Rep from * for desired length. Fasten off.

COLUMN 2 (and subsequent columns)

*With RS facing and A, cast on 12 sts, pick up and k11 sts along RH side of square 1. Rep rows 1–21. Rep from * for desired length, picking up sts along side of next square.

greek spiral

This is a two-color geometric pattern that felts beautifully and that can be used as an overall pattern, an insert or an edging.

Colors A (light) and B (dark)
(multiple of 10 sts plus 2)
Note On RS rows sl sts wyib, on WS rows, sl st wyif.
Row 1 (RS) With A, knit.

Row 2 With A, purl.

Row 3 With B, k1, *k8, sl 2; rep from *, end k1.

Row 4 With B, p1, *sl 2, p8; rep from *, end p1.

Row 5 With A, k1, *sl 2, k4, sl 2, k2; rep from *, end k1.

Row 6 With A, p1, *p2, sl 2, p4, sl 2; rep from *, end p1.

Row 7 With B, k1, *k2, sl 2, k4, sl 2; rep from *, end k1.

Row 8 With B, p1, *sl 2, p4, sl 2, p2; rep from *, end p1.

Row 9 With A, k1, *sl 2, k8; rep from *, end k1.

Row 10 With A, p1, *p8, sl 2; rep from *, end p1.

Row 11 With B, knit.

Row 12 With B, purl.

Row 13 With A, *k4, sl 2, k4; rep from *, end k2.

Row 14 With A, p2, *p4, sl 2, p4; rep from * to end.

Row 15 With B, k2, *sl 2, k2, sl 2, k4; rep from * to end.

Row 16 With B, *p4, sl 2, p2, sl 2; rep from *, end p2.

Row 17 With A, *k4, sl 2, k2, sl 2; rep from *, end k2.

Row 18 With A, p2, *sl 2, p2, sl 2, p4; rep from * to end.

Row 19 With B, *k6, sl 2, k2; rep from *, end k2.

Row 20 With B, p2, *p2, sl 2, p6; rep from * to end.

Rep rows 1–20.

This stylish charcoal-grey bag is inspired by the Op Art movement of the 1960s.

FINISHED MEASUREMENTS

Before felting

Approx 23"/53cm W x 15"/38cm H x 7½"/19cm D

After felting

Approx 20"/51cm W x 9½"/24cm H x 6½"/16.5cm D

MATERIALS

2 4oz/113g (approx 190yd/174m) of Brown Sheep Company's **Lamb's Pride Worsted** in #M06 deep charcoal

1 skein each #M03 grey heather (A) and #M04 charcoal heather (B)

2 Leisure Arts **Exclusively You** 27"/68.5cm single purse handles in #28309 black

1 Leisure Arts magnetic snap

2 wood dowels

Size 11 (8mm) needles

GAUGE

10 sts and 15 rows = 4"/10 cm in St st chart pattern using size 11 (8mm) needles and 2 strands of yarn held tog before felting

NOTE Two strands of yarn are held together throughout.

BAG

Front

With A, cast on 58 sts. Work in St st for 1¾"/4.5cm.

K next WS row for turning ridge.

K 1 row.

Cont in St st for for 1¾"/4.5cm. Work 37 rows of chart.
With A, work in St st for 4 rows.

Base

K next WS row for folding ridge.

K 1 row.

Cont in St st for 6½"/16.5cm.

K next WS row for folding ridge.

Back

K 1 row.

Work in St st for 3 rows.

Work 37 rows of chart.

With A, cont in St st for 1¾"/4.5cm.

K next WS row for turning ridge.

K 1 row.

Cont in St st for 1¾"/4.5cm. Bind off.

Weave in ends.

Sides

With RS facing and A, pick up 20 sts between folding
ridges at base of bag. Work in St st until same length
as front to turning ridge. K next WS row. K 1 row. Cont
in St st for 1¾"/4.5cm. Bind off. Rep on other side of
base.

FINISHING

Sew sides to front and back. Sew hems down.

Pocket

With A, cast on 20 sts. Work in St st for 5"/12.5cm. Bind
off firmly. Center pocket and sew in place.

Felt according to instructions on p. 8. When bag is
thoroughly dry, sew on handles as pictured. Attach
magnetic snap to center top edge. Insert dowels in
front and back hems.

19 18 17 16 15 14 13 12 11 10 9 8 7 6 5 4 3 2 1
10-st repeat

Color Key

■ MC

□ A

□ B

duplicate stitch

Duplicate-stitch embroidery is worked on stockinette stitch after the piece is knit and before it is felted. Knit your piece loosely, but not so loosely that it becomes difficult to work the duplicate stitch. In some cases, depending on the yarn gauge, you may still be able to see the duplicate stitch after the background is completely felted. (See Techniques for embroidery how-tos.)

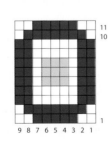

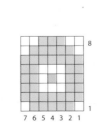

Color Key

☐	MC
☐	A
■	B
☐	C

embroidery

Included here is a nice mix of feltable embroidery stitches, added before felting. Many embroidery stitches felt well, and adding them can give a piece more life and character. The look of the embroidery changes after felting, so repeat the process until you achieve the look you want. The swatch shown here still shows the embroidered stitches after felting. Once more through the machine and the stitch definition would disappear—also a lovely look.

paisley palette

This swatch uses a combination of cord and embroidery applied before felting. Be sure to secure your French knots firmly so they will withstand the felting process.

Colors A, B, C, D, E and F

With A, make a 4-st I-cord (see Techniques) to length required for paisley outline. Fasten off and sew to fabric. Add embroidery following diagram (see Techniques).

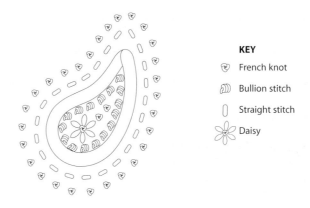

KEY

🌀 French knot

🌀 Bullion stitch

◖ Straight stitch

✿ Daisy

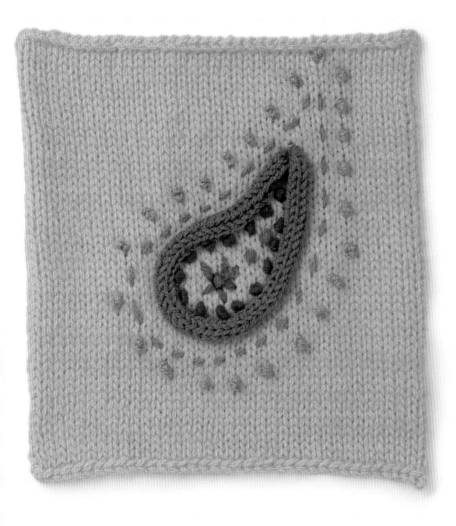

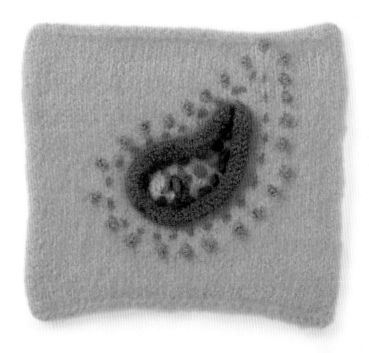

floral coat

This loose-fitting felted coat with tapestry floral motifs is embroidered in duplicate stitch and has I-cord frog closures and buttons.

KNITTED MEASUREMENTS
After felting
Bust (closed) 44 (48)"/111.5 (122)cm
Length 33"/83.5cm
Upper arm 14½"/37cm

MATERIALS
• 24 (25) .88oz/25g ball (each approx 82yd/75m) of Jamieson's/Simply Shetland **Shetland DK** (wool) in #880 coffee (MC)
• 1 ball each in #794 eucalyptus and 1190 burnt umber
• 1 2oz/57g ball (each approx 170yd/155m) of Jamieson's/Simply Shetland **Shetland DK** (wool) each in #230 yellow ochre, #821 rosemary, #365 chartreuse, #587 madder, #526 spice, #540 coral, #1190 burnt umber, #1140 granny smith, #147 moss, #794 eucalyptus and #769 willow
• One pair each sizes 8 and 9 (5 and 5.5mm) needles OR SIZE TO OBTAIN GAUGE
• Two size 8 (5mm) dpn

GAUGE
Before felting
17 sts and 24 rows = 4"/10cm over St st using larger needles.
After felting
18 sts and 29 rows = 4"/10cm.
TAKE TIME TO CHECK GAUGE.

tip
This is the big league: Do not make this coat as your first felting project!

BACK

With smaller needles and MC, cast on 100 (108) sts. K 4 rows. Change to larger needles. Next row (RS) Knit. Next row K2, p to last 2 sts, k2. Rep last 2 rows 14 times more. Work all sts in work St st for 175 rows above 4 garter rows.

Armhole shaping

Bind off 1 (5) sts at beg of next 2 rows, 2 sts at beg of next 4 rows. Dec 1 st each side every other row 3 times—84 sts. Work even until armhole measures 9½"/24cm.

Shoulder shaping

Bind off 9 sts at beg of next 6 rows. Bind off rem 30 sts for back neck.

RIGHT FRONT

With larger needles and MC, cast on 30 (34) sts. K 1 row, p 1 row. Cast on 4 sts at beg of next RS row, k to end. P 1 row. Rep last 2 rows 2 times more—42 (46) sts. Cast on 2 sts at beg of next RS row, k to end. Rep last 2 rows 2 times more—48 (52) sts. Work even until there are 175 rows from beg. Shape armhole at side edges only as for back—40 sts. Work even through chart row 212.

Neck and shoulder shaping

Next row (RS) Bind off 8 sts (neck edge), work to end. Cont to bind off from neck edge 2 sts once, then dec 1 st every other row 3 times, AT SAME TIME, when same length as back to shoulder, shape shoulder at side edge as for back.

LEFT FRONT

With A and large needles, cast on 30 (34) sts. K 1 row. Cast on 4 sts at beg of next WS row, p to end. K 1 row. Rep last 2 rows 2 times more—42 (46) sts. Cast on 2 sts at beg of next WS row, p to end. K 1 row. Rep last 2 rows 2 times more—48 (52) sts. Cont to work to correspond to right front, reversing shaping.

Right front band

With RS facing, smaller needles and MC, pick up 240 (245) sts evenly along lower and front edge of right front. K 4 rows. Bind off.

Left front band

Work same as right front band.

SLEEVES

With smaller needles and MC, cast on 46 sts. K 4 rows. Change to larger needles. Work in St st, inc 1 st each side every 4th row 6 times and every 6th row 4 times—66 sts. Work even until there are 86 rows from beg.

Cap shaping

Bind off 5 sts at beg of next 2 rows, 2 sts at beg of next 4 rows. Dec 1 st each side every other row 16 times. Bind off 2 sts at beg of next 2 rows. Bind off rem 12 sts.

FINISHING

Sew shoulder seams.

Collar

With RS facing, larger needles and MC, pick up 23 sts along right neck edge, pick up 24 sts on back neck edge, pick up 3 sts along left neck edge—70 sts. Work St st for 11 rows. P 1 row on RS. P next row. Cont in St st for 10 rows. Bind off. Work all duplicate stitch and embroidery following charts for colors and motif placement. Note Use a mirror image of the right front chart when embroidering the left front.

Set in sleeves. Sew side and sleeve seams. Sew collar to inside edge.

Cord frog closures

With dpn and MC cast on 3 sts. *Next row (RS) K3. Do not turn work, slide 3 sts to beg of needle to work next row from RS; repeat from * to desired length. Make three 25"/63.5cm long cords (21"/53cm after felting). Make three 6" long cords for buttons (3½"/9cm after felting). **Note** Fold cord several times and put a loose rubber band around it to keep it from tangling.

Felting

Wash coat in machine on hot/cold cycle with a pair of jeans. Repeat until desired size is achieved. Felt as before.

Follow diagram to make frogs. Sew frogs to right front, the first one just below neck shaping and the other two spaced 8"/20.5cm apart.

Buttons

Make a square knot (left over right and right over left) and sew ends together. Sew buttons on left side opposite frogs.

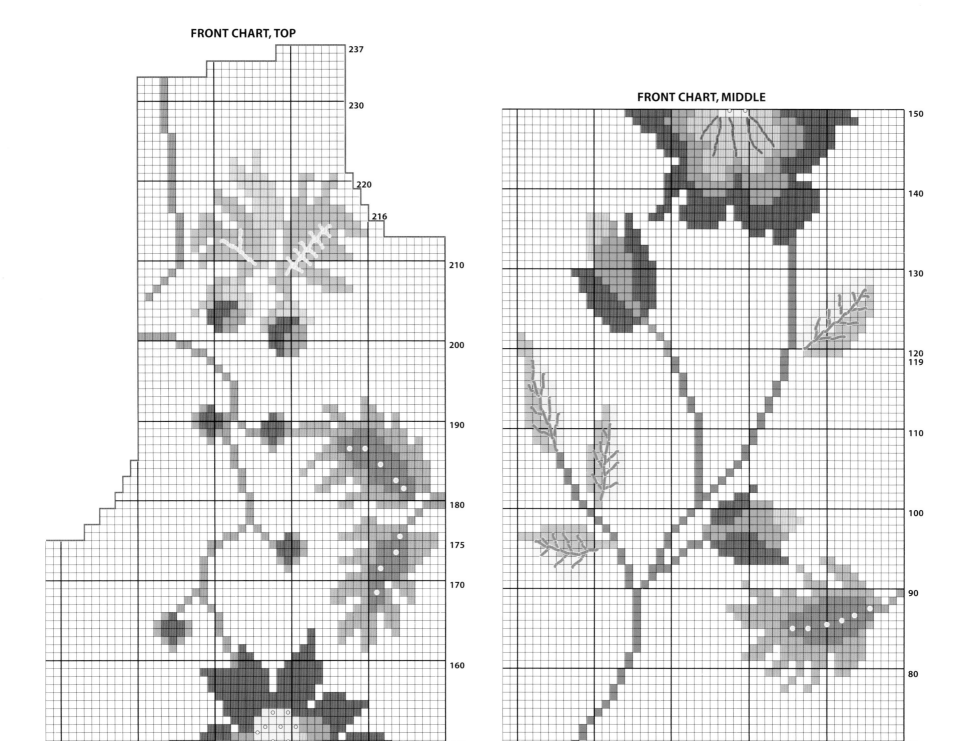

FRONT CHART, TOP

237
230
220
216
210
200
190
180
175
170
160
150

FRONT CHART, MIDDLE

150
140
130
120
119
110
100
90
80
71

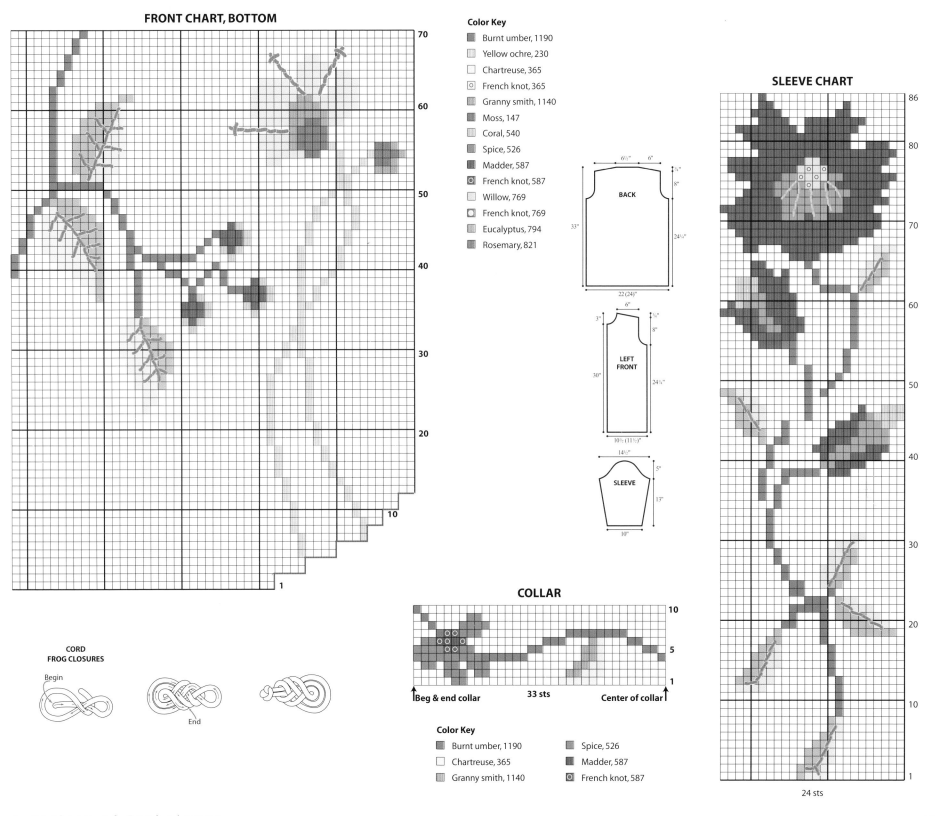

FRONT CHART, BOTTOM

70
60
50
40
30
20
10
1

Color Key

- Burnt umber, 1190
- Yellow ochre, 230
- Chartreuse, 365
- ⊙ French knot, 365
- Granny smith, 1140
- Moss, 147
- Coral, 540
- Spice, 526
- Madder, 587
- ⊙ French knot, 587
- Willow, 769
- ⊙ French knot, 769
- Eucalyptus, 794
- Rosemary, 821

BACK

6½" 6"
¾"
8"
33"
24¼"
22 (24)"

LEFT FRONT

6"
3" ¾"
8"
30"
24¼"
10½ (11½)"

SLEEVE

14½"
5"
13"
10"

SLEEVE CHART

86
80
70
60
50
40
30
20
10
1

24 sts

CORD
FROG CLOSURES

Begin

End

COLLAR

10
5
1

Beg & end collar   33 sts   Center of collar

Color Key

- Burnt umber, 1190
- Chartreuse, 365
- Granny smith, 1140
- Spice, 526
- Madder, 587
- ⊙ French knot, 587

thistle embroidery

❶ Colors A, B, C, D, E and F

With A, work in St st for background. Add embroidery following diagram (see Techniques). Felt according to instructions on p. 8.

sunflower embroidery

❷ Colors A, B, C, D, E and F

With A, work in St st for background. Add embroidery following diagram (see Techniques). Felt according to instructions on p. 8.

❶

❷

combining yarns

You can achieve an unusual look by combining a natural fiber with a synthetic fur. This combination works with many other novelty yarns if you use them sparingly as stripes or edging for a piece.

beaded knitting

There are a few things to remember when using knitted-in beads. Choose beads made of a washable material, such as glass, certain plastics or unpainted wood. Do a swatch to make sure the beads you've chosen will work. And be sure to keep the size of the bead and yarn in mind so the bead doesn't get lost in the felting.

wool and fur

❶ Colors A (wool) and B (fur)
(Any number of sts)
Cast on with A.
Rows 1–14 With A, work in St st.
Rows 15 and 16 With B, work in st st.

Rep rows 1–16 for desired length less ½"/1.3cm.
With B, work in St st for 4 more rows.
Bind off.

beads

❷ (multiple of 6 plus 5)
Note String beads onto yarn before casting on.
PB (place bead) Slide bead to RH needle, k next

st slipping bead through st on LH needle and keeping bead at back of work.
Row 1 (RS) *K5, PB; rep from *, end k5.

Row 2 Purl.
Row 3 K2, *PB, k5; rep from *, end last rep k2.
Row 4 Purl.
Rep rows 1–4.

woven drop stitch

The first swatch shows the effect of weaving a novelty yarn through the dropped stitches before felting. Novelty yarns do not felt but can be used in small amounts for accents. The second swatch shows a drop-stitch pattern without the novelty yarn woven through.

woven vertical ladders

Colors A (main) and B (contrast)

(multiple of 7 sts)

Cast on with A.

Row 1 (RS) K2, *bind off 3 sts, k3; rep from *, end last rep k1.

Row 2 P2, *pick up and k1 st over bound-off sts, p4; rep from *, end last rep p2.

Row 3 K2, p1, *k4, p1; rep from *, end k2.

Row 4 P2, k1, *p4, k1; rep from *, end p2.

Rep rows 3 and 4 until 2 rows from desired length.

Next row K2, *drop next st, cast on 3 sts, k4; rep from *, end last rep k2.

Last row Purl.

Bind off. Unravel dropped sts to cast-on edge. Weave strands of B through ladders.

drop stitch

(multiple of 5 sts plus 1)

Work in St st for desired length.

Next row (RS) K5, *drop next st, cast on 1 st, k4; rep from *, end k1.

Bind off.

Unravel dropped sts to cast-on edge.

❶

❷

entrelac

This longtime classic technique felts nicely, flattening out in the process. A self-striping yarn would work beautifully.

entrelac

Colors A and B
(multiple of 12 sts)

Inc 1 K in front and back of next st.
With A, cast on loosely.

Base triangles

With A, *p2 (WS), turn and k2, turn and p3, turn and k3, turn and p4, turn and k4, cont in this manner working 1 more st every WS row until "turn and p12" has been worked; rep from * to end. Break off A.

First row of rectangles

With B, k2, turn and p2, turn and inc 1, skp, turn and p3, turn and inc 1, k1, skp, turn and p4, turn and inc 1, k2, skp, turn and p5, turn and inc 1, k3, skp, turn and p6, cont in this manner working 1 more st every RS row until "inc 1, k9, skp" has been worked (edge triangle). Cont as foll: *pick up and k12 sts along edge of next triangle, [turn and p12, turn and k11, skp] 12 times (rectangle); rep from * to edge of last triangle, pick up and k12 sts along edge of last triangle, turn and p2tog, p10, turn and k11, turn and p2tog, p9, turn and k10, turn and p2tog, p8, turn and k9, cont in this manner until "turn and k2" has been worked, turn and p2tog—1 st

rem. Break off B.

Second row of rectangles

With A, pick up and p11 sts along edge of trangle just worked, [turn and k12, turn and p11, p2tog] 12 times, then cont as foll: *pick up and p12 sts along side of next rectangle, [turn and k12, turn and p11, p2tog] 12 times; rep from * to end. Break off A.

Third row of rectangles

Work same as first row except pick up sts along side of rectangles.
Rep second and third rows.

Final row of triangles

With A, *pick up and p11 sts along edge of triangle just worked, turn and k12, turn and p2tog, p9, p2tog, turn and k11, turn and p2tog, p8, p2tog, turn and k10, turn and p2tog, p7, p2tog, cont in this manner, working 1 st less every WS row until "turn and k3" has been worked, turn and [p2tog] twice, turn and k2, turn and p1, p2tog, p1, turn and k3, turn and p3tog; rep from * picking up sts along side of rectangle. Fasten off.

❶

edgings

Edgings always add a crowning touch to any knitted piece. Here are a few felted edgings from my books *Knitting On the Edge*, *Knitting Over the Edge* and *Knitting Beyond the Edge*.

❷

holsters

❶ (multiple of 4 sts plus 4)

Work 4 rows in garter st.

Row 1 (RS) P4, *turn, cast on 8 sts, turn, p4; rep from * to end.

Row 2 K4, *p8, k4; rep from * to end.

Row 3 P4, *k8, p4; rep from * to end.

Rows 4, 6 and 8 Rep row 2.

Rows 5, 7 and 9 Rep row 3.

Row 10 K4, *bind off 8 sts purlwise, k4; rep from * to end.

Row 11 Purl.

Row 12 Knit.

Cont as desired.

open tubes

❷ À (multiple of 3 sts plus 3)

Work 2 rows in garter st.

Row 1 (RS) P3, *turn, cast on 5 sts, turn, p3; rep from * to end.

Row 2 K3, *p5, k3; rep from * to end.

Row 3 P3, *k5, p3; rep from * to end.

Rows 4, 6, 8, 10, 12 and 14 Rep row 2.

Rows 5, 7, 9, 11, 13 and 15 Rep row 3.

Row 16 K3, *bind off 5 sts purlwise, k3; rep from * to end.

Row 17 Purl.

Row 18 Knit.

Cont as desired.

jester's points

(multiple of 27 sts plus 15)

Notes Each point is worked separately, then all points are joined on the same row. Cut yarn on all but last point and leave sts on needle.

MB (make bobble) [K1, p1, k1, p1, k1] in next st, [turn, k5] 4 times, pass 2nd 3rd, 4th and 5th sts over first st.
Cast on 2 sts.

Row 1 (RS) Knit.

Row 2 Yo, k to end—3 sts.

Row 3 Yo, k to end—4 sts.

Row 4 Yo, k to end—5 sts.

Row 5 Yo, k to end—6 sts.

Row 6 Yo, k to end—7 sts.

Row 7 Yo, k to end—8 sts.

Row 8 Yo, k to end—9 sts.

Row 9 Yo, k to end—10 sts.

Row 10 Yo, k to end—11 sts.

Row 11 Yo, k to end—12 sts.

Row 12 Yo, k to end—13 sts.

Row 13 Yo, k to end—14 sts.

Row 14 Yo, k to end—15 sts.
Cut yarn and leave sts on needle.
On same needle, cast on and work rows 1 through 11 (12 sts) to make another point. Cont in this manner until desired number of points are made, ending with a 15-st point and leaving sts on spare needle.
To join points, knit across sts of all points on needle. Work 2 rows garter st.

Next row (RS) K2, *MB, k5; rep from *, end last rep k3.
Work 5 rows in garter st.
Cont as desired.

tip

For textural interest, combine felted and unfelted knitting. For example, add a felted edging to an unfelted piece.

5
appliqués, cords and bag handles

In this chapter, I'll show you some special touches that you can use to bring your felted projects to vibrant and creative life: appliqués of colorful flowers, a selection of leaves and even autumnal acorns that will add unique adornments to your projects. You'll also find cord projects that can be the main design element or the edging of your work. And, since felted bags are perennially popular on the fashion scene, I've included patterns for eight fabulous felted handles that will complement your favorite handbag.

114

appliqués

Flowers, leaves and berries make exciting additions to any piece, and I've included a wide variety in this chapter. These appliqués can be felted separately and applied to any kind of piece, either felted or unfelted, or they can be applied first and then felted along with the piece. I usually felt the appliqués by hand if I sew them on them afterwards, because these small elements sometimes need extra hand agitation. Then, after hand felting, I put them in a laundry bag and felt them in the washing machine. In some cases, attaching the appliqués after felting gives you more flexibility, allowing you to see how the background felts before you make final placement decisions. However, sewing the appliqués onto the piece before felting can also work. As a general rule, if the appliqués and the body of the piece are made out of the same yarn, it's safe to felt them together. If they're made out of different yarns, you might want to felt them separately.

Felting by hand

To felt by hand, you will need liquid laundry detergent, rubber gloves, towels, a bowl of very hot water and a bowl of ice water. Add a small amount of laundry detergent to the hot water, submerge the knitted appliqués and let them soak for a few minutes. Then rub the pieces vigorously for about five minutes.

Dip the pieces into the cold water and continue rubbing. Repeat the hot and cold rubbing until the pieces are felted as desired. Finally, use cool water to gently rinse any remaining soap out of the pieces. Roll the felted pieces in a terry cloth towel to remove excess water. Shape the pieces and allow them to dry on a flat surface.

twisted roses & leaves

Colors A and B

ROSE

With A, cast on 66 sts.

Rows 1 and 3 (RS) Knit.

Rows 2 and 4 Purl.

Row 5 *K6, rotate LH needle counterclockwise 360 degrees; rep from * to end.

Row 6 Purl.

Row 7 *K2tog; rep from * to end—33 sts.

Row 8 *P2tog; rep from *, end p1—17 sts.

Row 9 *K2tog; rep from *, end k1—9 sts.

Cut yarn, leaving a long tail. Thread tail through rem 9 sts on needle, pull tightly and secure. Twist rose into a spiral and stitch to hold spiral in place securely so it can withstand the felting process. You will need to twist and reshape the rose after it is felted.

LEAF (make 2 or 3)

With B, cast on 5 sts.

Row 1 (RS) K2, yo, k1, yo, k2—7 sts.

Rows 2, 4 and 6 Purl.

Row 3 Ssk, k3, k2tog—5 sts.

Row 5 Ssk, k1, k2tog—3 sts.

Row 7 SK2P—1 st.

Fasten off.

Felt in the washing machine (see p. 8) or by hand (see this page). For machine felting, place the pieces in a laundry bag. Sew leaves to base of rose where desired.

from my readers

Huge success! I knitted and felted all the flowers for my wedding. I wanted a knitted bouquet so I could have an everlasting keepsake that would retain color and not wilt or gather dust like silk flowers. I also wanted something that I wouldn't have to pay an arm and a leg for. I looked all over the Internet and my local yarn store for patterns or images to go by, but found absolutely nothing. Then, Nicky Epstein's Knitted Flowers was published. It took a little extra creative ingenuity on my part to turn the patterns into a bouquet, but the results were fabulous and I got rave comments.

—Kristy Lucas

lilacs & leaves

Colors A and B

LILAC

With A, make a slip knot.

*Cast on 4 sts, bind off 4 sts, sl rem st to LH needle; rep from * 6 times more. Fasten off. Thread cast-on tail through top loops of slipped sts, pull tightly and secure. Make knot for flower center, pull tightly and secure on WS.

LEAF

With B, cast on 9 sts.

Rows 1, 3 and 5 (RS) K3, S2KP, k3—7 sts.

Rows 2 and 4 K1, m1, k2, p1, k2, m1, k1—9 sts.

Row 6 K3, p1, k3.

Row 7 K2, S2KP, k2—5 sts.

Row 8 K2, p1, k2.

Row 9 K1, S2KP, k1—3 sts.

Row 10 K1, p1, k1.

Row 11 S2KP—1 st.

Fasten off.

Felt in the washing machine (see p. 8) or by hand (see p.115). For machine felting, place the pieces in a laundry bag.

unfelted

acorns & leaves

Colors A, B and C

ACORN

Base

With A, cast on 5 sts, leaving a long tail for seaming.

Row 1 (RS) [K in front and back of st] 5 times—10 sts.

Rows 2, 4, 6, 8 and 10 Purl.

Rows 3, 5, 7, 9 and 11 Knit.

Row 12 P1, [p in front and back of st] 8 times, p1—18 sts.

Top

Rows 13 and 14 With B, knit.

Rows 15–20 Work in rev St st.

Row 21 P1, [p2tog] 8 times, p1—10 sts.

Row 22 [K2tog] 5 times—5 sts.

Cut yarn, leaving a long tail. Thread tail through rem sts on needle, gather and fasten securely, then make a 2"/5cm chain. Stuff lightly with fiberfill. With cast-on tail, gather cast-on edge, sew seam and fasten off.

ACORN LEAF

Stem

With C, cast on 5 sts.

Row 1 (RS) K1, [sl 1, k1] twice.

Row 2 Sl 1, [p1, sl 1] twice.

Rep rows 1 and 2 for 1"/2.5cm.

Leaf

Row 1 (RS) *K1, m1; rep from *, end k1—9 sts.

Rows 2, 4, 6, 10, 12 and 16 Purl.

Row 3 *K1, m1; rep from *, end k1—17 sts.

Row 5 Knit.

Row 7 Bind off 3 sts, k to end—14 sts.

Row 8 Bind off 3 sts, p to end—11 sts.

Rows 9 and 11 Knit.

Row 13 Bind off 3 sts, k to end—8 sts.

Row 14 Bind off 3 sts, p to end—5 sts.

Row 15 Ssk, k1, k2tog—3 sts.

Row 17 SK2P—1 st.

Fasten off.

With B, using stem st, embroider veins on leaves. Felt in the washing machine (see p.8) or by hand (see p.115). For machine felting, place the pieces in a laundry bag.

unfelted

palm leaves

autumn leaf

cherry leaves

I knitted a bag, using Noro/KFI Kureyon, which felts like crazy, but because I had no access to a washing machine, I tried felting it by hand.

How hard could it be? I filled the sink with water, dropped the bag in, and started wringing away. I scrubbed, twisted, even tried using the ribbed handgrip of a broom to get the stuff to full (felt). All I had to show for my efforts were a sore back, aching arms and a slightly fuzzy bag. I tried again, by dropping it in the shower and stomping on it. I rubbed and smooshed the thing around...again to no avail.

Time passed. Last night, I washed some socks in the sink, caught a glimpse of the bag, and had a thought. I can make handspun yarn felt just from accidentally swishing it around a little too much while setting it, but I can't full a stupid bag? I wonder...

Grabbed the bag. Grabbed the soap. Got the water really hot, then plunged the whole thing in. This time, however, there was no scrubbing, just swishing around, a gentle pedaling motion with the fabric held loosely in my hands. Triumphant, I lifted the perfectly fulled bag from the water. So don't kill yourself when felting by hand. Just pretend that what you're working with is an heirloom sweater that must not felt. Treat it gently, and the thing will shrink up in no time.

—Jenny Bannock

palm leaf

Colors A and B
With A, cast on 3 sts.
Rows 1, 3 and 5 (RS) K in front and back of st, k to last st, k in front and back of st —9 sts.
Rows 2 and 4 Purl.
Rows 6–14 Work in St st.
Rows 15, 17 and 19 Ssk, k to last 2 sts, k2tog — 3 sts.
Rows 16 and 18 Purl.
Row 20 SK2P—1 st.
Fasten off.
With B, using stem st, embroider veins on leaves. Felt in the washing machine (see p. 8) or by hand (see p.115). For machine felting, place the pieces in a laundry bag.

autumn leaf

Colors A and B
SSP [Sl 1 knitwise] twice, sl both sts back onto LH needle, p2tog tbl.
SP2P Sl 1 knitwise, p2tog, psso.
With A, cast on 2 sts.
Row 1 (RS) K1, m1, k1—3 sts.
Rows 2, 4, 5, 8 and 12 Purl.
Row 3 K1, [m1, k1] twice—5 sts.
Row 5 K1, [m1, k1] 4 times — 9 sts.
Row 7 [K2, m1] twice, k1, [m1, k2] twice— 13 sts.
Row 9 Bind off 2 sts, k10—11 sts.
Row 10 Bind off 2 sts, p8—9 sts.
Row 11 Knit.
Rows 13–24 Rep rows 7–12 twice.
Row 25 Ssk, k5, k2tog—7 sts.
Row 26 P2tog, p3, SSP— 5 sts.
Row 27 Ssk, k1, k2tog—3 sts.
Row 28 SP2P—1 st.
Fasten off.
With B, using stem st, embroider veins on leaves. Felt in the washing machine (see p. 8) or by hand (see p.115). For machine felting, place the pieces in a laundry bag.

cherry leaf

Colors A and B
SP2P Sl 1 knitwise, p2tog, psso.
With A, cast on 5 sts.
Row 1 (RS) K2, yo, k1, yo, k2—7 sts.
Row 2, 4, 6, 8, 10 and 12 Purl.
Row 3 K3, yo, k1, yo, k3—9 sts.
Row 5 K4, yo, k1, yo, k4—11 sts.
Row 7 Ssk, k7, k2tog—9 sts.
Row 9 Ssk, k5, k2tog—7 sts.
Row 11 Ssk, k3, k2tog—5 sts.
Row 13 Ssk, k1, k2tog—3 sts.
Row 14 SP2P—1 st.
Fasten off.
With B, using stem st, embroider veins on leaves. Felt in the washing machine (see p. 8) or by hand (see p.115). For machine felting, place the pieces in a laundry bag.

Following are examples of floral appliqués on a lace and a textural background. The swatches are shown both unfelted and felted.

bird's-eye roses & leaves

❶ Colors A (background), B and C (Multiple of 4 sts)

Cast on with A.

Row 1 (WS) *K2tog, [yo] twice, k2tog; rep from * to end.

Row 2 *K1, [k1, p1] into double yo, k1; rep from * to end.

Row 3 K2, *k2tog, [yo] twice, k2tog; rep from *, end k2.

Row 4 K2, *k1, [k1, p1] into double yo, k1; rep from *, end k2.

Rep rows 1–4.

Rose

With B, cast on 10 sts.

Row 1 (RS) Knit.

Row 2 and all WS rows Purl.

Rows 3, 5 and 7 *K in front and back of st; rep from * to end.

Row 8 Purl

With B, bind off.

Leaf

Make 2.

With 2 strands C held tog, make a slip knot. Cast on 5 sts, bind off 5 sts. Slip rem st to LH needle. Cast on 8 sts, bind off 8 sts. Fasten off rem st.

Sew leaves onto rose. Sew roses onto fabric where desired. Felt in the washing machine (see p. 8) or by hand (see p.115). For machine felting, place the pieces in a laundry bag.

cording stitch flowers

❷ Colors A (background), B, C and D (Any number of sts)

Cast on with A.

Rows 1, 3, 5 and 7 (RS) Knit.

Rows 2, 4 and 6 K1, p to last st, k1.

Row 8 K1, *wyif insert RH needle into top of next purl st 4 rows below, pick up loop and place on LH needle and p together with next st; rep from * to last st, k1.

Rep rows 1–8.

Flower

With B or C, cast on 35 sts.

Row 1 (RS) *K1, bind off 5 sts (2 sts on RH needle); rep from * to end —10 sts.

Cut yarn and thread tail through rem sts on needle. Pull tightly and secure. With D, attach flowers where desired while embroidering flower centers. Felt in the washing machine (see p. 8) or by hand (see p.115). For machine felting, place the pieces in a laundry bag.

cherries jubilee slippers

These whimsical slippers are sized to fit most adults' feet.

SIZES
S (M, L, XL)

FINISHED MEASUREMENTS
Before felting
Approx 12½ (13 ½, 14, 16)"/31.5 (34.5, 35.5, 40.5)cm L

After felting
Approx 9½ (10, 10 ½, 12)"/24 (25.5, 26.5, 30.5)cm L

MATERIALS
• 3 3½ oz/100g balls (223yd/204m) Patons **Classic Merino Wool** (wool) in #00240 leaf green (A)
• 1 ball each #205 deep olive (B) and #230 bright red (C)
• Size 10.5 (6.5mm) needles
• Tapestry needle

GAUGE
16 sts and 18 rows = 4"/10cm over St st using size 10.5 (6.5mm) needles with a single strand before felting.

Quaker pattern
Rows 1 and 3 (RS) Purl.
Rows 2 and 4 Knit.
Rows 5 and 7 Knit.
Rows 6 and 8 Purl.
Rep rows 1–8.

Sole
Starting at heel with 2 strands A, cast on 5 (6, 7, 8) sts. Working in garter st, inc 1 st at beg of next 6 rows. Cont in garter st on 11 (12, 13, 14) sts until piece measures 7 (7, 7½, 7½)"/18 (18, 19.5, 19.5)cm from beg. Inc 1 st at beg of next 4 (4, 6, 6) rows. Work even on 15 (16, 19, 20) sts until piece measures 12 (13, 13, 15)"/30.5 (33, 33, 38)cm from beg. Dec 1 st at beg of next 6 (6, 8, 8) rows. Bind off rem 9 (10, 11, 12) sts.

Foot
Using one strand of A, cast on 111 (117, 123, 135) sts. Work in Quaker pat for 20 rows.

Shape instep
Row 1 (RS) K59 (62, 65, 71), k2tog, turn.
Row 2 Sl 1, p7, p2tog, turn.
Row 3 Sl 1, k7, ssk, turn.
Rep rows 2 and 3 until there are 28 (30, 32, 34) sts left on each side of center 9 instep sts, end with a WS row, turn. Sl 1, k to end of row, turn. P to last 2 sts, p2tog—64 (68, 72, 76) sts. Work in 1x1 rib for 3"/7.5cm.

Cuff
Row 1 (RS) K, inc 10 sts evenly across – 74 (78, 82, 86) sts.
Row 2 (turning ridge) Knit.
Row 3 Join B. P2 B, *k2 A, p2 B; rep from * to end.
Row 4 K2 B, *p2 A, k2 B; rep from * to end.
Rep rows 3 and 4 until piece measures 3"/7.5cm from turning ridge. Bind off all sts.

FINISHING
Sew center back seam. With RS tog, sew foot to sole. Turn RS out and turn cuff down.

Leaves (make 6)
With 2 strands B, cast on 9 sts.
Rows 1, 3 and 5 (RS) K3, S2KP, k3—7 sts.
Rows 2 and 4 K1, m1, k2, p1, k2, m1, k1 — 9 sts.
Row 6 K3, p1, k3.
Row 7 K2, S2KP, k2—5 sts.
Row 8 K2, p1, k2.
Row 9 K1, S2KP, k1—3 sts.
Row 10 K1, p1, k1.
Row 11 S2KP—1 st.
Fasten off.

Stems and cherries (make 2 of each)
MC (Make Cherry) [K in front, back, front, back, front] of next st, p1 row, k 1 row, p 1 row, k2tog, k1, k2tog, turn. P3tog. Fasten off.

Double cherry
With 1 strand B, cast on 14 sts, bind off 13 sts. With C, MC. Fasten off.
MC at opposite end of stem. Fasten off.

Single cherry
With 1 strand B, cast on 8 sts, bind off 7 sts. With C, MC. Fasten off.

Felt all pieces according to instructions, placing leaves and cherries in a laundry bag. Fold stem of double cherry and sew to cuff at front of slipper together with end of single cherry. Sew 3 leaves at base of stems.

cords

Cords are knitted separately and then sewn onto a piece. You can apply the cords to the background before or after felting. When felting cords, always put them into a laundry bag, which will prevent them from tangling and twisting around other pieces you may be felting or the jeans you use for agitation. Following are a few different ideas: a simple cord appliquéd before felting into a daisy shape, cords tied to a background to form loops and cord applied after felting to form a celtic scroll. The next pair of swatches shows a fringe and an interesting bar cord technique. One of my favorites is the fishtail frog, shown later in this chapter on a contrasting background. (For more frogs formed from I-cord, see my book Knitting Beyond the Edge.)

When making cords, use two double-pointed needles or one short circular needle, unless otherwise indicated. The cords are made separately, then sewn onto the piece. If you sew on the cord, use a tapestry needle and the same yarn used to make the cord. Pin the cord in place on top of the fabric. Using small running stitches, work from the right or wrong side, catching the cord with each stitch.

I-cord flowers

❶ Work background in St st, using self-striping or variegated yarn. Make 4-st I-cord (see Techniques) to desired length, using the same yarn. Sew cord to background foll diagram. Felt according to instructions on p.8.

loops

❷ (Any number of sts)
Rows 1 and 3 (WS) Purl.
Row 2 Knit.
Row 4 *K in front and back of st; rep from * to end.
Row 5 *K2tog; rep from * to end.
Row 6 Knit.

Rep rows 1–6.

Loops
Make desired number of 4-st I-cords (see Techniques) in desired lengths. Using cast-on and bind-off tails, sew ends to adjacent ridges. Felt according to instructions on p. 8.

celtic scroll pillow

SIZE

Before felting

Approx 19"/48.5cm W x 55"/140cm L

After felting

Approx 16"/40.5cm W x 34"/86.5cm L

FINISHED MEASUREMENT

Approx 16"/40.5cm square

MATERIALS

• 4 skeins 3½oz/100g balls (each approx 183yd/167m) of Tahki Donegal Tweed Homespun in #866 dark gray
• Size 10.5 (6.5mm) needles
• Size 9 (5.5mm) dpns
• Three corresponding buttons
• One 16"/40.5cm square pillow form

GAUGE

16 sts and 20 rows = 4"/10cm over St st using 10.5 (6.5mm) needles before felting.

PILLOW

Cast on 73 sts and work in St st until piece measures 55"/140cm. Bind off.

CORD

With dpns, cast on 5 sts. Work four I-cords (see Techniques) for 17"/43cm.

FINISHING

Fold piece widthwise, leaving a 6"/15cm flap. Sew side seams. Felt according to instructions on p.8, placing cords in laundry bag.

Pin cords in place following diagram and sew to pillow front.

Sew 3 buttons evenly across opening at pillow back approx 1"/2.5cm from edge. Cut 3 holes on flap to correspond with buttonholes. Insert pillow form and button flap.

seed stitch/cord scroll

Work fabric in seed st, using self-striping yarn, and felt according to instructions on p.8. Using same yarn, make a 3-st I-cord (see techniques) approximately 34"/86.5cm in length. Sew cord to fabric foll photo, hiding ends under a crossing.

fishtail frog

Make two 3-st I-cords (see techniques) to required length. Felt according to instructions on p. 8. Form frogs using T-pins to anchor (beg with the cast-on edge) on an ironing board or on a piece of Styrofoam board at least 10"/25.5cm square.

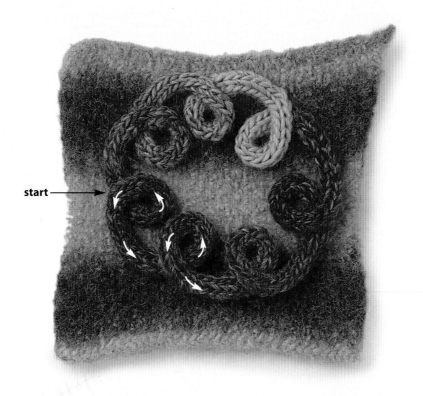

start →

tip

If you are sewing cord to a piece after the cord is felted, use sewing thread for easier stitching.

•start
•end

bridged cord

(multiple of 5 sts)
Work in St st for 2"/5cm or desired length.
*Using dpns, k5, work I-cord on these sts only to desired length (see Techniques), and place sts on holder.

Join yarn to next st and rep from * for rem sts. Place all sts from holder onto knitting needle with RS facing. Join yarn and work in St st for 2"/5cm.
Felt according to instructions on p. 8.

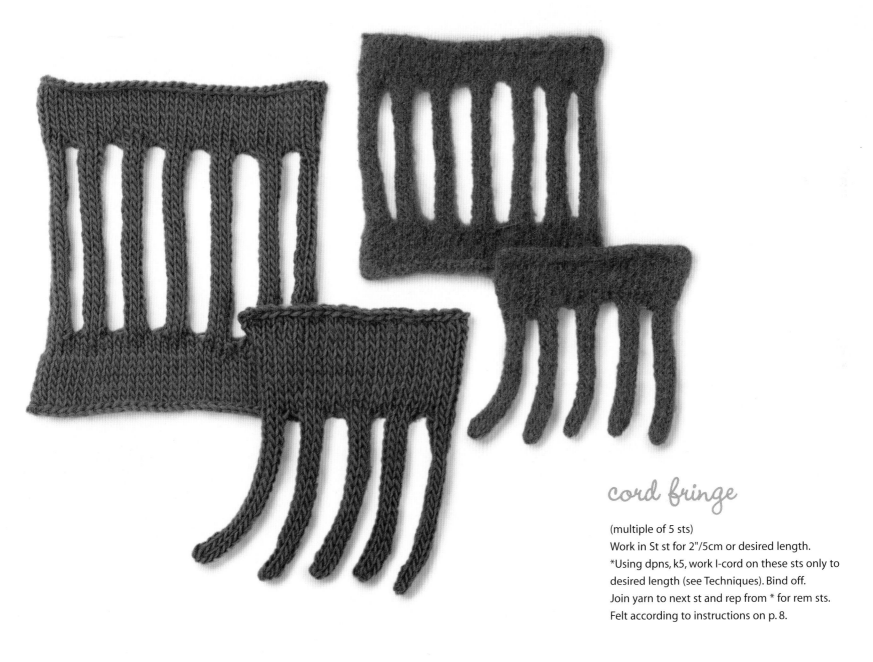

cord fringe

(multiple of 5 sts)
Work in St st for 2"/5cm or desired length.
*Using dpns, k5, work I-cord on these sts only to desired length (see Techniques). Bind off.
Join yarn to next st and rep from * for rem sts.
Felt according to instructions on p. 8.

bag handles

Shown here are eight bag handles made using a variety of fun techniques. All are sturdy enough to support a knitted handbag. The techniques include twisting, braiding, knotting and looping cord and cables. All of these pieces should be placed in a laundry bag before felting. You will find resources for hardware on p.176.

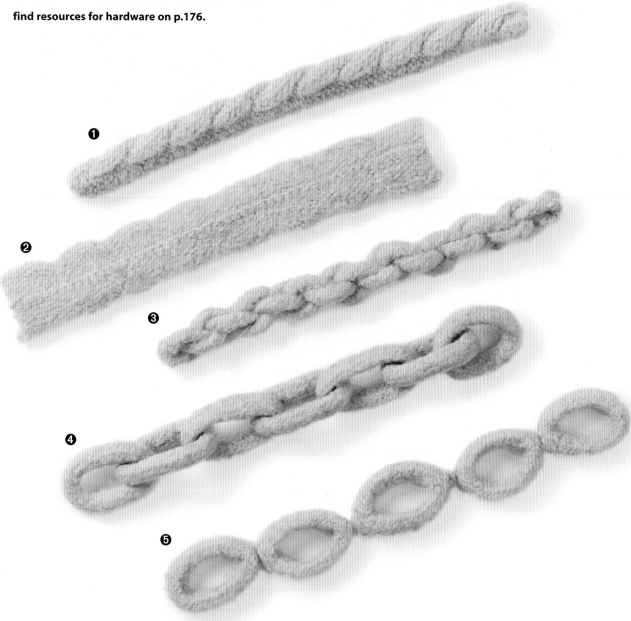

❶ cable
(worked over 12 sts)
6-st RC Sl 3 sts to cn and hold to back, k3, then k3 from cn.
Rows 1, 3 and 5 (WS) K3, p6, k3.
Row 2 P3, k6, p3.
Row 4 P3, 6-st RC, p3.
Row 6 Rep row 2.
Rep rows 1–6 for desired length.
Felt according to instructions on p.8.

❷ t-twist stockinette stitch
Make 2.
Cast on a multiple of 6 sts plus 4 sts for desired length.
Rows 1–6 Work in St st, beg with a k row.
Row 7 (RS) K2, *k6, rotate the LH needle counterclockwise 360 degrees; rep from *, end k2.
Rows 8–11 Work in St st, beg with a p row.
Place sts on a spare needle and make 2nd piece.
With RS tog, join the 2 pieces using 3-needle bind off (see Techniques). Felt according to instructions on p.8.

❸ twisted cord
Make two 5-st I-cords (see Techniques) to desired length.
Felt according to instructions on p.8.
Twist cords together (see Techniques). Sew ends together to secure.

❹ chain link cord
*Cast on 8 sts using provisional cast-on (see Techniques). Work in St st for 5" or desired length for link, ending with a RS row. Join to cast-on sts with 3-needle bind off or Kitchener st (see Techniques). Fasten off and flip RS out. Rep from * for desired number of links, slipping cast-on end through previous link before joining ends.
Felt according to instructions on p.8.

❺ roundabout
*Cast on 8 sts using provisional cast-on (see Techniques). Work in St st for 5" or desired length for link, ending with a RS row. Join to cast-on sts with 3-needle bind off or Kitchener st (see Techniques). Fasten off and flip RS out. Rep from * for desired number of links.
Felt according to instructions on p.8. Sew links together end to end.

❻ knot cord

Make two 5-st I-cords (see Techniques) to desired length. Felt according to instructions on p.8. Holding both cords together, make an overhand knot every 5"/12.5cm or as desired.

❼ plain cord

Cast on 10 sts. Work in St st for desired length. Felt according to instructions on p.8. Letting side edges of fabric roll naturally to the WS, sew seam to form a tube.

❽ braided cord

Make three 5-st I-cords (see Techniques) to desired length. Felt according to instructions on p.8. Join 3 cords together at one end. Braid and sew ends together to secure.

from my readers

Here is my tip for making I-cord handles sturdy and stretch resistant yet nicely soft and flexible. In the plumbing department of your local hardware store, purchase 1/8" vinyl tubing to insert through the inside of your knitted I-cord before felting. Punch a hole across each end of the tubing to secure the ends of the I-cord, using the tails from the cast-on and bind-off. Leave about 1/4" of I-cord extending past the vinyl tubing at each end. Felt as usual, placing the handles in a separate mesh laundry bag so they don't interfere with the felting of the bag. After felting, it's easy to sew the handles on through the yarn-covered ends. I really like these handles and often use this method even when purchased handles are suggested. It is extremely economical, too, as the vinyl tubing is only about twenty cents a foot!

—Diane Freeman

6
cut it out!

My goal in this chapter is to inspire you to cut up your knitting. Remember when you were a small child and you enjoyed cutting shapes out of colored paper? Perhaps you made stars, flowers and animals that you then used to create original works of art. Well, in this chapter you'll be using felted knit fabric instead of colored paper, but your goal will be the same: to cut out pieces that can stand on their own or be appliquéd to other pieces. All you need is fabric adhesive or a needle and thread, plus a template. You can create your template from designs you find in art books, coloring books or other sources of inspiration, or you can use the ones in this book. I've chosen a few of my favorite shapes to help you get started. In this chapter and at the back of the book, you'll find templates for animals, flowers, leaves, stars, apples and a unique cut-and-twist flower that I call a Cutting Edge Mumsy. Once you have your template, place it on your felted piece, grab your favorite scissors, pin, and cut away in a frenzy of unbounded creativity. In no time, you'll have the prettiest design that ever was.

When knitting a piece to use for a cutting project, think big. Make sure your knitted piece is two to three times the size of the template you plan to use to allow for shrinkage during felting. The great thing about felted knitting is that it will not unravel. So cut away!

Cutting is also a wonderful way to make something from a boo-boo. If a felted piece has gone wrong, it can enjoy a creative rebirth with just a few judicious snips of the scissors. I created some of my most beautiful flowers from felted pieces that did not quite come out as planned.

In addition to projects made from templates and patterns, this chapter includes a variety of cut edgings, fringes, woven pieces, holes with grommets and cut buttonholes. I hope that seeing all of these examples will open your eyes to many creative possibilities.

templates

To make felted pieces from templates, follow these simple procedures:

1. Knit a flat piece of stockinette stitch in the color or colors you'd like. Make sure the knitted pieces are at least two to three times larger than the total size of the templates.

2. Felt the knitted piece or pieces according to the directions on p.8.

3. Dry the piece or pieces flat.

4. Photocopy and cut out the appropriate templates (see pages 160–172). Lay the template on the felted piece, pin and cut.

5. Following the assembly template, sew or use fabric adhesive to assemble the felted piece.

6. Add embroidery or beads as shown in the photo and assembly template.

winter and summer

❶ Template pp. 160-161

spring tulip garden

❷ Template pp. 162-163

tip

Photocopy the template before cutting it out! This allows you to reduce or enlarge it.

❶

Pointsettia

Sunflower

❷

cutting edge mumsy

❶ Cut out a felted rectangle approximately 1½" by 8". Cut parallel slits along one long edge approximately ¼" apart, ending about ¼" from opposite edge. Roll the uncut edge to form a spiral, and sew to hold flower shape.

You can adjust the size of the rectangle to make different size flowers.

cut felted flowers

❷ Template p. 164

animal friends

❸ Template pp. 165-167

Here is a great idea for projects that just didn't turn out right: When one of my felted prototypes fails to meet my standards, I refuse to let all of that knitting and lovely wool go to waste. I take out my large circular (about 4–5 inches) cookie-cutter and use it to trace out as many circles as possible without overlapping. Throw the circles in the washer for a quick run so that the edges felt a bit. Lay the wet circles out side-by-side on a towel. Place something flat and heavy over them to make sure they dry flat. A cookie sheet with a heavy mixing bowl on top of it works well. Once the circles are dry, you have a great set of felted coasters. Stacked up neatly and tied with a lovely ribbon, they make a great gift.

—Jennifer Pace

❸

❶

pretty posie

❶ Template p. 167

cut beaded stars

❷ Template p. 168

delicious

❸ Template p. 168

autumn

❹ Template p. 169

❷

tip

You can use many of these cut designs for holiday ornaments by adding a string or ribbon tie to the top. They make great gifts for teachers or friends.

❸

❶

basketweave

❶ Basketweave is great for pillows, scarves, potholders or bags. You will need two solid-colored pieces of felting. Cut one piece into strips of the desired length and width. In the other piece, cut slits the width of the strips, the desired width apart. Weave the strips into the background piece, alternating placement as shown.

grommets and buttonholes

❷ Grommets Grommets can be used as holes for handles or as decorative elements. You can purchase grommets at hobby or sewing-supply stores (see Resources). Follow package directions for attaching grommets.

❸ Buttonholes You can add buttons and buttonholes to any felted piece by simply sewing the buttons on and cutting slits for buttonholes.

❷

❸

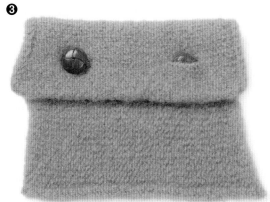

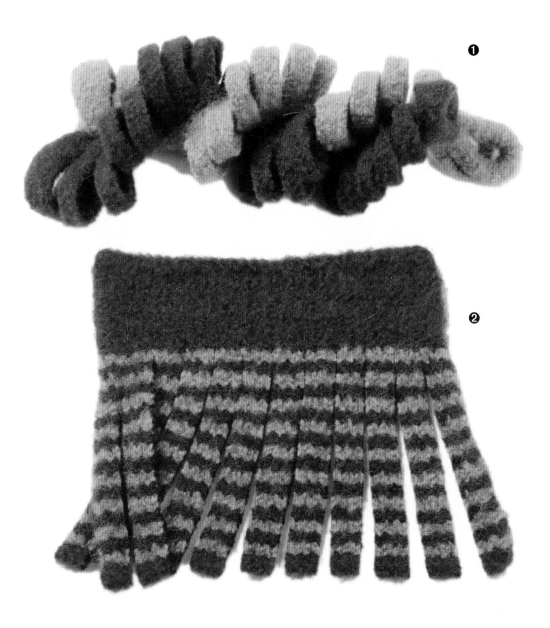

curly q

❶ This can be used as an edging or a scarf.

1. Cut a long, narrow rectangle of felt. Fold each side (long) edge toward the center. Pin and stitch down on each side.

2. Cut each folded side evenly in parallel cuts, spaced $1/2$" apart. Each cut should extend from the outer edge to within $1/4$" of the center stitching.

3. Twist the resulting fringe to form curlicues. Sew curls in place to secure.

striped fringe

❷ Colors A and B. With A, cast on desired number of sts. Purl one row.

Row 2 (RS) With A, k across.

Row 3 (WS) With B, p across.

Repeat Rows 2 and 3 for stripe pattern to desired length. Change to solid color, if desired, and work remainder of piece. Felt as described on p.8. After felting, cut even strips of desired width through the stripe pattern.

dots

Negative Dots (left) are made by cutting holes in one felted piece and attaching that piece to a background so that the background color shows through.

1. Make two pieces of felt in different colors.
2. Choose a round object in the size you want—for example, a coin or a jar lid—and trace its outline on paper. Place the template on the felted piece and cut dots in the desired pattern. To cut a small circle, use sharp scissors to poke a hole into the center of each dot and then cut carefully around the outline.
3. Glue or sew the cut piece of felt to the solid background.

Positive Dots (right) are made by gluing dots onto a solid-color background. Both techniques can be used for bags, place mats, potholders or other decorative objects.

The dots on the right swatch are shown in different colors, but you can use just one color or many. To make the swatch:

1. Make pieces of felt in desired colors.
2. Make a circle template (see Negative Dots), and cut out dots.
3. Glue or sew dots to background as desired.

tip

We've used dots here to create this fanciful look. But you can cut out any shape you choose. Cut the see-through shapes into any felted piece to give your scarf, handbag, or other projects a personal, unique and avant-garde design.

pointy border

round border

everything old is new again

Another great way to employ the felt-and-cut technique is to start with an old sweater or knitted piece from your closet or one that you've found in a flea market or thrift shop. Felt it and you've got a fabulous new background to cut up into delicious designs. On the following pages, I show old knitted pieces used to create new felted ones. I've hand-sewn a fish and Christmas stocking and machine-sewn a toy horse, bunny, slippers and bag using Vogue patterns. The pattern numbers are listed for you, but you can certainly use different printed patterns or even patterns you design yourself.

When choosing old sweaters, whether hand- or machine-knitted, be sure to pick garments that are made of wool or other animal fibers and that have colors you like. Also remember that stitch patterns may get lost in the felting process.

christmas stockings

To make these Christmas stockings, use the template on page 170.

1. Choose a hand- or machine-knitted sweater, and felt according to the instructions on p.8. To be sure you will have enough material to make the stockings, choose a sweater that is at least two to three times larger than the amount of fabric you will need.

2. Cut and sew, following the pattern.

3. Add jingle bells and ribbed cuff as shown.

tip

If your sweater doesn't have ribbing, cut out a scalloped or pointed edge (see p. 136). Be inventive!

baby slippers

To make these baby slippers, use Vogue Pattern #7717.

1. Choose a hand- or machine-knitted sweater, and felt according to the instructions on p.8. To be sure you will have enough material to make the slippers, choose a sweater that is at least two to three times larger than the amount of fabric you will need.

2. Cut and sew, following the pattern.

3. Add ribbon, lace or ribbed cuffs as shown.

green fair isle bag

To make the bag, use Vogue Pattern V8214A.

1. Choose a hand- or machine-knitted sweater, and felt according to the instructions on p. 8. For this bag, I used pieces of two different sweaters that looked good together. To be sure you will have enough material, choose a sweater or sweaters that are at least two to three times larger than the amount of fabric you will need.

2. Cut and sew, following the pattern.

3. Add handle as shown.

fish

To make the fish, use the template on page 171.

1. Choose a hand- or machine-knitted sweater, and felt according to the instructions on p.8. To be sure you will have enough material to make the fish, choose a sweater that is at least two to three times larger than the amount of fabric you will need.

2. Cut and sew, following the template. Let the sweater you use inspire the way you design your felted piece. For example, I used the sweater's ribbed edges for the fish's fins. If your sweater has no ribbing, use part of the sweater body instead.

3. Add eyes and mouth cut out of scraps of the sweater as shown.

toy horse and bunny

To make either the horse or the bunny, use Vogue Pattern 7760.

1. Choose a hand- or machine-knitted sweater, and felt according to the instructions on p.8. To be sure you will have enough material, choose a sweater that is at least two to three times larger than the amount of fabric you will need.

2. Cut and sew, following the pattern.

5-in-1 sweater projects

Create five projects out of one old sweater. That's recycling with flair!

Separate cardigan into 1 back, 2 fronts and 2 sleeves.

PROJECT 1: MAN'S HAT
FINISHED MEASUREMENTS

23"/58.5cm circumference 9"/23cm diameter uncuffed

Working with the sweater back, snip a strand halfway up and unravel to separate. Continue to unravel 2 complete rows, picking up sts with a spare needle. K2tog across row, p2tog across row, k2tog across row. Thread end of unraveled strand through rem sts, gather tightly and secure. Cont to sew seam on WS to 3"/7.5cm from bottom edge, then turn hat right side out and finish sewing seam for cuff. Felt according to instructions on p. 8.

PROJECT 2: WOMAN'S HAT
FINISHED MEASUREMENTS

22"/56cm inner circumference 7½"/19cm diameter

ADDITIONAL MATERIALS

• 2 layers of 26"/66cm x 14"/35.5cm quilt batting
• Sewing needle and thread

Working with the upper half of the sweater back, unravel 2 complete rows, picking up sts with a spare needle. Complete same as for man's hat. Roll batting into a 3¼"/8.5cm diameter cylinder and stitch in place with needle and thread. Bring ends together to form a ring and sew securely. Roll brim to outside of hat, inserting batting. With unraveled yarn, sew edge in place 7"/17cm from top of hat, easing edge in

place to enclose batting and shape brim. Brim should fit loosely around batting to allow for shrinkage. Felt according to instructions on p.8.

ANGEL ROSE
FINISHED MEASUREMENTS

4¼"/11cm diameter

Felt sleeve according to instructions on p. 8. Using templates (see page 172), cut 5 petals and 1 center piece. Form spiral beg with short side in, stitch in place. Fold and stitch each petal at bottom center. Sew 5 petals around center. Sew above brim of hat.

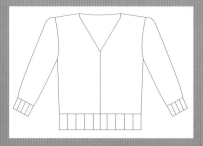

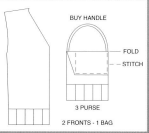

BUY HANDLE

FOLD

STITCH

3 PURSE

2 FRONTS - 1 BAG

SNAP

Fold

DOG SWEATER   SLEEVE RIB

1 SLEEVE - 1 DOG SWEATER

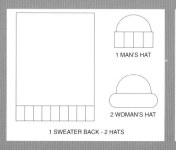

1 MAN'S HAT

2 WOMAN'S HAT

1 SWEATER BACK - 2 HATS

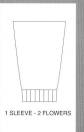

1 SLEEVE - 2 FLOWERS

PROJECT 3: PURSE

FINISHED MEASUREMENTS

10½"/26.5cm W x 9"/23cm H

ADDITIONAL MATERIALS

• One Leisure Arts Exclusively You 27" moc croc purse handle

Working with both sweater fronts, place pieces RS together. Starting at base of neck shaping, sew side and bottom seams. Turn RS out and fold yoke down, then fold shoulder edge up to meet opening. Sew sides of yoke to form a pocket. Rep on other side. Felt according to instructions. Sew purchased purse strap at side seams.

PROJECT 4: DOG SWEATER

FINISHED MEASUREMENTS 13½"/34.5cm L x 10"/25.5cm W buttoned and uncuffed (cuff = 1½"/4cm diameter)

Felt sweater sleeve according to instructions. Fold in half lengthwise. Cut a buttonhole at one corner of shoulder edge. Fold shoulder edge to fit and sew button opposite buttonhole.

PROJECT 5: DAHLIA

FINISHED MEASUREMENTS

6"/15cm diameter

Felt sweater sleeve according to instructions. Using templates (see page 172) cut 12 petals and circle. Using circle as the base, sew 6 petals at center for bottom layer, 6 for top layer. Place top layer on bottom so petals alternate. Cut a piece 6" x 1"/15 x 2.5cm for center. Make ½"/1.25cm cuts across top every ¼"/.64cm. Roll to form spiral and sew to center of petals. Sew purchased bead fringe around spiral and sew bead at center.

7
sculptural felting

Sculptural felting is the creation of unique three-dimensional pieces that will add charm and whimsy to your home. Some pieces, such as the lovely Sherwood Forest bowl are freestanding. Others are stuffed with polyester filling or quilt batting to achieve the three-dimensional look.

Small sculptural pieces can be stuffed before felting, while larger pieces work better if they are stuffed after felting. If you stuff before felting, be careful to avoid overstuffing to allow for shrinkage. You can always cut the item, put in more stuffing and sew it up after it is felted. Also, if you decide to stuff the piece after felting, make sure you leave an opening in the piece. Flexibility is a wonderful aspect of felting.

For this chapter I've created food-inspired dimensional pieces such as a felted fruit bowl (an unusual centerpiece), and the Sherwood Forest bowl, which would look beautiful beside a fireplace or on a mantel. So let's start stuffing and felting!

vegetables

Create a beautiful Della Robbia wreath by adding the fruits or vegetables to a purchased wreath. Most craft stores carry a variety of wreaths to choose from.

MATERIALS

3 3½oz/100g skeins (each approx 137yd/123m) of Manos del Uruguay/The Design Source **Handspun Multi Colors** (wool) in #101 jungle multi (A)

2 skeins **Handspun Semi Solids** each in #E english (B), #Z straw (F) and #38 aster (H)

1 skein each in #13 green (C), #69 hibiscus (D), #66 poppy red (E), #58 marigold (G), #14 natural (I), #K putty (J) (small amount), #37 thrush (K) (small amount), #W persimmon (L) and #55 olive (M)

One pair size 11 (7mm) needles OR SIZE TO OBTAIN GAUGE

Size 9 (5.5mm) dpns

Quilt batting (2 layers) 48"/122cm x 62"/157.5cm

Fiberfill stuffing

Twelve 2"/5cm binder clips (for peppers)

Tapestry needle

Long sewing needle and thread—any color

GAUGE

12 sts and 19 rows = 4"/10cm over St st using size 11 (7mm) needles, before fulling.

TOMATO

(make 3)

Note Knit in 2 sections. Make 2 pieces for each tomato.

With D, cast on 8 sts.

Rows 1 and 3 (RS) Knit.

Rows 2 and 4 Purl.

Row 5 K1, *m1, k1; rep from * to end—15 sts.

Row 6 Purl.

Row 7 K in front and back of next st, *m1, k1; rep from * to last st, k in front and back of last st—31 sts.

Rows 8–22 Work in St st.

Row 23 K1, *k2tog; rep from * to end—16 sts.

Rows 24–26 St st.

Row 27 *K2tog; rep from * to end—8 sts.

Row 28 Purl.

Row 29 *K2tog; rep from * to end—4 sts.

Cut yarn, leaving a long tail. Thread tail through rem sts and fasten securely. Sew one side seam, stuff lightly and sew 2nd seam. Gather top and bottom edges and sew closed.

Stem

With K, cast on 8 sts. K 1 row. Bind off.

Collar

With M, *cast on 6 sts, bind off 5 sts; rep from * 5 times more—6 sts on needle. [K2tog] 3 times—3 sts. SK2P—1 st. Fasten off.

Center collar circularly onto top of tomato and sew in place. Sew stem to center of collar. Felt according to instructions on p.8.

PEPPER

(make 2 E and 1 G)

With E (G), cast on 30 sts.

Row 1 Knit.

Row 2 Purl.

Rows 3 and 4 (short rows) K20, turn, p to end.

Row 5–10 Work in St st.

Rep rows 1–10 eight times more.

Bind off. Sew cast-on and bind-off rows together. Stuff lightly and gather side edges (top and bottom of pepper) and sew closed with C.

Stem

With C and dpn, cast on 4 sts. Work in I-cord (see Techniques) for 2"/5cm. Bind off. Sew to top of pepper.

Felt according to instructions on p.8. Pinch 4 vertical sections of pepper body with binder clips and let dry completely before removing.

ZUCCHINI

(make 1)

With C, cast on 65 sts.

Rows 1 and 3 (RS) Knit.

Rows 2 and 4 Purl.

Row 5 (short row) K50, turn.

Row 6 Purl.

Row 7 (short row) K32, turn.

Row 8 Purl.

Rows 9 and 10 With I, work in St st.

Rows 11–14 With C, work in St st.

Rep rows 2–14 five times more.

Bind off. Sew side seam, leaving a 5"/12.5cm opening.

Stem

With C, cast on 5 sts.

Rows 1 and 3 (WS) Purl.

Rows 2 and 4 K1, m1, k to last st, m1, k1.

Rows 5–8 Work in St st.

Rows 9 and 11 Purl.

Rows 10 and 12 K1, k2tog, k to last 3 sts, ssk, k1.

Stuff lightly and sew side seam. Gather top and bottom edges and sew closed. Sew securely to top (narrow end) of zucchini. Felt according to instructions. Stuff lightly with fiberfill and sew remainder of seam closed.

EGGPLANT

(make 2)

With H, cast on 36 sts.

Row 1 (RS) Knit.

Row 2 Purl.

Row 3 (short row) K20, turn.

Row 4 Purl.

Rows 5 and 6 Work in St st.

Row 7 (short row) K30, turn.

Row 8 Purl.

Rep rows 1–8 ten times.

Bind off. Sew side seam leaving a 5"/12.5cm opening.

Leaf

(make 4)

With M, cast on 3 sts.

Row 1 (WS) Purl.

Row 2 K in front and back of st, k to last st, k in front and back of st.

Rows 3–6 Rep rows 1 and 2.

Row 7 Purl.

Row 8 Ssk, k to last 2 sts, k2tog.

Rows 9–12 Rep rows 7 and 8.

Row 13 Purl.

Row 14 SK2P.

Fasten off.

Stem

With M, RS facing and dpn, pick up and k2 sts at cast-on edge of each leaf—8 sts.

Next row *P2tog; rep from * to end—4 sts.

Work in I-cord (see Techniques) for 3"/7.5cm. Bind off. Sew to top of eggplant.

Felt according to instructions on p. 8. Stuff lightly and sew remainder of seam closed.

CORN

(make 3)

Ladder seed st (multiple of 2 sts):

Row 1 *K1, p1; rep from * to end.

Row 2 Knit.

Cob

With F, cast on 12 sts.

Rows 1–4 Work in Ladder seed st.

Row 5 K1, *m1, work 2 sts in Ladder seed st; rep from *, end m1, p1—18 sts.

Rows 6–8 Work in Ladder seed st.

Row 9 K1, *m1, work 3 sts in Ladder seed st; rep from *, end m1, k1, p1—24 sts.

Rows 10–12 Work in Ladder seed st.

Row 13 K1, p1, *m1, work 4 sts in Ladder seed st; rep from *, end m1, k1, p1—30 sts.

Rows 14–23 (dec) Work in Ladder seed st, dec 1 st each end of row—10 sts.

Row 24 *K2tog; rep from * to end—5 sts.

Row 25 K2tog, k1, ssk—3 sts.

Row 26 SP2P—1 sts.

Fasten off.

Stuff lightly and sew side seam.

Husk

With B, cast on 14 sts.

Rows 1 and 3 (RS) Knit.

Rows 2 and 4 Purl.

Row 5 K2, *m1, k2; rep from * to end—20 sts.

Rows 6–8 Work in St st.

Row 9 K2, *m1, k3; rep from * to end—26 sts.

Rows 10–12 Work in St st.

Row 13 K2, *m1, k4; rep from * to end—32 sts.

Rows 14–41 Work in St st for 28 rows.

Rows 42–52 Work in St st, dec 1 st each end of row—10 sts.

Row 53 *K2tog; rep from * to end—5 sts.

Row 54 P2tog, p1, p2tog—3 sts.

Row 55 SK2P—1 st.

Fasten off.

Beg at cast-on edge, sew edges of husk together for 4"/10cm. Sew base of cob securely to base of husk. Felt according to instructions on p. 8.

Silk

Cut 10"/25cm strands of F and J. Fold in half and attach to top of cob. Trim as desired.

CARROT

(make 4)

With L, cast on 26 sts. [K 1 row, p 1 row. Short rows: K to last 6 sts, turn, p to end. K to last 12 sts, turn, p to end. K to last 18 sts, turn, p to end] 3 times. K 1 row. Bind off purlwise. Stuff lightly and sew seam. Gather top seam and sew closed.

Stems

With C, make a slip knot. *Cast on 8 sts, bind off 8 sts, sl rem st to LH needle**, cast on 5 sts, bind off 5 sts, sl rem st to LH needle; rep from * until there are two 5-st stems and three 8-st stems. Gather sl st edge and sew to top of carrot. Felt according to instructions on p. 8.

ONION

(make 4)

With I, follow instructions for Tomato, making only 1 section for each. Stuff lightly and sew side seam. Gather top and bottom edges and sew closed.

Scapes

With B, cut two or three 6"/15 strands for each onion. Fold strands and loop through top of onion for stems. Felt according to instructions on p. 8.

GARLIC

(make 5)

With I, cast on 4 sts.

Row 1 (RS) Knit.

Row 2 Purl.

Row 3 Kfb every st—8 sts.

Rows 4–6 Work in St st.

Row 7 K2, *m1, k1; rep from * to end—14 sts.

Row 8 Purl.

Row 9 K2, *m1, k3; rep from * to end—18 sts.

Rows 10–16 Work in St st.

Row 17 K2tog, k to last 2 sts, k2tog—16 sts.

Rows 18–20 Work in St st.

Row 21 *K2tog; rep from * to end—8 sts.

Row 22 Purl.

Row 23 *K2tog; rep from * to end—4 sts.

With J and dpns, work I-cord (see Techniques) for 2"/5cm on 3 garlics, 3"/7.5cm on 1 garlic and 4"/10cm on 1 garlic.

Stuff lightly and sew side seam. Gather bottom edge and sew closed, adding ends for roots if desired. Felt according to instructions on p. 8.

bowl of fruit

MATERIALS

1 4oz/113g skein (approx 190yd/173m) of Brown Sheep Company **Lamb's Pride Worsted** (wool/mohair) in #M08 wild oak (A)

1 skein each #M155 lemon drop (B), #M110 orange you glad (C), #M120 limeade (D), #M69 old sage (E), #M07 sable (F), #M28 chianti (G) and #M56 clematis (H)

Size 8 (5mm) dpns

1 bowl in desired shape, for mold

Fiberfill

Tapestry needle

GAUGE

18 sts and 24 rows = 4"/10cm over St st using size 8 (5mm) needles

BOWL

FINISHED MEASUREMENTS

Before felting

Approx 5½"/14cm H x 10"/25.5cm Diameter (across top of bowl)

After felting

Approx 4"/10cm H x 8"/20cm diameter (across top of bowl)

With A, cast on 5 sts. Work in I-cord (see Techniques) for approx 210"/533.5cm, keeping sts on needle (in order to add or subtract length) until bowl is finished. Starting at bottom center of bowl with cast-on end of cord, begin to coil cord around bowl, stitching together at the same time. When shaping is complete, bind off cord. With F, work blanket st over coils at lower half of bowl.

Felt according to instructions on p. 8. Shape bowl while wet.

PEACH

With B, cast on 3 sts.

Row 1 (RS) [K1, m1] twice, k1—5 sts.

Rows 2, 4, 6 and 8 Purl.

Rows 3, 5 and 7 *K1, m1; rep from *, end k1—33 sts after row 7.

Row 9 K1, *k8, m1; rep from *, end k1—37 sts.

Row 10 P14 B, join C and p9 C, join 2nd strand B and p14 B.

Row 11 K11 B, k15 C, k11 B.

Row 12 P8 B, p21 C, p8 B.

Row 13 K7 B, k23 C, k7 B.

Row 14 P6 B, p25 C, p6 B.

Row 15 K5 B, k27 C, k5 B.

Row 16 P4 B, p29 C, p4 B.

Row 17 K3 B, k31 C, k3 B.

Row 18 P2 B, p33 C, p2 B.

Row 19 With B, knit.

Row 20 Bind off 6 sts, k to end—31 sts.

Row 21 Bind off 6 sts, p to end—25 sts.

Row 22 *K2tog; rep from *, end k1—13 sts.

Row 23 *P2tog; rep from *, end p1—7 sts.

Row 24 Rep row 22—4 sts.

Row 25 With A, [k2tog] twice—2 sts. Bind off.

Stuff lightly and sew seam. Felt according to instructions on p. 8.

Leaf

(make 2)

With D, cast on 3 sts.

Row 1 (RS) Kfb, k1, kfb—5 sts.

Row 2 Purl.

Row 3 K1, kfb, k1, join E and [kfb, k1]—7 sts.

Rows 4 and 6 P3 E, p4 D.

Row 5 With k4 D, p3 E.

Row 7 With D, [ssk, k2], with E [k1, k2tog]—5 sts.

Row 8 P2 E, p3 D.

Row 9 With D [ssk, k1], with E [k2tog]—3 sts.

Row 10 P1 E, p2 D.

Row 11 SK2P E—1 st.

Fasten off.

Sew leaves to base of stem. Felt according to instructions on p. 8.

ORANGE

With C, cast on 5 sts.

Row 1 (WS) [K1, m1] 4 times, k1—9 sts.

Rows 2, 4, and 6 Purl.

Rows 3 and 5 *K1, m1; rep from *, end k1—33 sts after row 5.

Row 7 *K5, m1; rep from *, end k3—39 sts.

Rows 8–18 Work in Reverse St st.

Row 19 *K5, k2tog; rep from *, end k4—34 sts.

Row 20 *P2, p2tog; rep from *, end p2—26 sts.

Row 21 *K2, k2tog; rep from *, end k2—20 sts.

Row 22 With B, *p1, p2tog; rep from *, end p2—14 sts.

Row 23 K1, *k2tog; rep from *, end k1—8 sts.

Row 24 With D, [p2tog] 4 times—4 sts.

Row 25 [K2tog] twice—2 sts.

Row 26 Cast on 2 sts—4 sts.

Bind off 4 sts for stem.

Thread cast-on tail through cast-on sts, stuff lightly and sew seam. Using A, embroider an "X" at base of orange. Felt according to instructions on p. 8.

PLUM

With G, cast on 3 sts.

Row 1 (RS) K1, m1, k1, m1, k1—5 sts.

Row 2 and all WS rows except Row 18 Purl.

Rows 3, 5 and 7 *K1, m1; rep from *, end k1—33 sts after row 7.

Rows 9–17 Work in St st.

Row 18 Bind off 4 sts, p to end—29 sts.

Row 19 Bind off 4 sts, k to end—25 sts.

Row 21 *K2tog; rep from *, end k1—13 sts.

Row 23 Rep row 21—7 sts.

Thread tail through rem sts, pull tight and secure. Using H, duplicate stitch one or two patches at center of plum if desired. Stuff lightly and sew seam.

Leaf

(make 2)

With D, cast on 9 sts.

Rows 1, 3 and 5 (RS) K3, S2KP, k3—7 sts.

Rows 2 and 4 K1, m1, k2, p1, k2, m1, k1—9 sts.

Row 6 K3, p1, k3.

Row 7 K2, S2KP, k2—5 sts.

Row 8 K2, p1, k2.

Row 9 K1, S2KP, k1—3 sts.

Row 10 K1, p1, k1.

Row 11 S2KP—1 sts.

Fasten off.

Sew leaves to top of plum. Felt according to instructions on p.8.

GRAPES

(make 36 with H, 5 with G)

Cast on 1 st.

Row 1 (RS) K in [front, back, front, back, front] of st—5 sts.

Rows 2 and 4 Purl.

Row 3 Knit.

Row 5 Ssk, k1, k2tog—3 sts.

Row 6 P3tog—1 st.

Fasten off.

Tie cast-on and bind-off tails together and tuck into grape using tapestry needle.

With A, sew grapes together starting with one at bottom and adding 2 more in each subsequent layer, stringing and sewing the grapes in circles.

Make a knot at the top. Cast on 6 sts, then bind off for stem.

Leaf

(make 2)

With E, cast on 5 sts.

Row 1 (RS) *Kfb, k1, yo, k1, yo, k1, kfb—9 sts.

Rows 2, 4, 6, 10, 12, 16 and 18 Purl.

Rows 3 and 9 K4, yo, k1, yo, k4—11 sts.

Rows 5 and 11 K5, yo, k1, yo, k5—13 sts.

Row 7 Bind off 3 sts, k2, yo, k1, yo, k6—12 sts.

Row 8 Bind off 3 sts, p8—9 sts.

Row 13 Bind off 3 sts, k9—10 sts.

Row 14 Bind off 3 sts, p6—7 sts.

Row 15 SKP, k3, k2tog—5 sts.

Row 17 SKP, k1, k2tog—3 sts.

Row 19 SK2P—1 st.

Fasten off.

Sew leaves to top of bunch. Felt according to instructions on p. 8.

BANANA

With D, cast on 5 sts.

Row 1 (RS) [K1, m1] 4 times, k1—9 sts.

Row 2 Purl.

Row 3 Join B. K1 with B, [k1 with D, m1 with B] 6 times, k1 with D, k1 with B—15 sts.

Rows 4 and 6 With B, purl.

Row 5 [K2, m1] 7 times, k1—22 sts.

Row 6 Purl

Row 7 Sl 1, k5, sl 1, k8, sl 1, k5, sl 1.

Row 8 Purl

Rep rows 7 and 8 until piece measures 8½"/21.5cm from beg,

end with a WS row.

Next row *K1 with D, k2tog with B; rep from *, end k1 with D—15 sts.

Next row With D, purl.

Next row *K2tog; rep from *, end k1—8 sts.

Next row With D, purl.

Next row K2tog, k to last 2 sts, k2tog—6 sts.

Work in I-cord (see Techniques) for 1"/2.5cm.

Next row [K2tog] 3 times—3 sts.

Next row Purl.

Last row SK2P—1 st.

Fasten off.

Stuff lightly and sew seam, pulling tightly to gather and form curve. Felt according to instructions on p. 8.

sherwood forest bowl

FINISHED MEASUREMENTS

Before felting

Approx 23½"/59.5cm W,
48"/122cm circumference

After felting

Approx 16½"/42cm W, 41"/104cm
circumference, 11"/28cm high

MATERIALS

• 8 skeins 3.5oz/100g balls (each
approx 110yd/100m) of Muench/
Naturwolle **Multi** (handspun wool)
in #8 Terra
Size 13 (9mm) circular needle
One set size 13 (9mm) dpns
Tapestry needle
Sewing needle and matching
thread

GAUGE

8 sts and 12 rows = 4"/10cm over
St st with 2 strands held together
using size 13 (9mm) needles,
before fulling.
TAKE TIME TO CHECK GAUGE.
Note Bowl is knit in the round
holding 2 strands together.

BOWL

Top

Cast on 50 sts and k 1 rnd. Pm and
join without twisting sts. Work in St
st for 4"/10cm.

Body

Next rnd K in front and back of
every st—100 sts.
Work in St st until piece measures
14"/35.5cm from beg.

Shape base

Change to dpns when necessary.
Rnd 1 *K2tog, k8; rep from *—
90 sts.
Rnd 2 and all even-numbered rnds
Knit.
Rnd 3 Knit.
Rnd 5 *K2tog, k7; rep from *—
80 sts.
Rnd 7 *K2tog, k6; rep from *—
70 sts.
Rnd 9 *K2tog, k5; rep from *—
60 sts.
Rnd 11 *K2tog, k4; rep from *—
50 sts.
Rnd 13 *K2tog, k3; rep from *—
40 sts.
Rnd 15 *K2tog, k2; rep from *—
30 sts.

Rnd 17 *K2tog, k1; rep from *—
20 sts.
Rnd 19 *K2tog; rep from *—10 sts.
Rnd 21 *K2tog; rep from *—5 sts.
Cut yarn leaving a tail. With
tapestry needle, thread end
through rem sts on needle. Gather
up and fasten securely.
Note Use single strand for leaves
and berries.

Leaves

(make 18)
Cast on 5 sts.
Row 1 (RS) K2, yo, k1, yo, k2—7 sts.
Rows 2, 4 and 6 Purl.
Row 3 K3, yo, k1, yo, k3—9 sts.
Row 5 K4, yo, k1, yo, k4—11 sts.
Row 7 Bind off 3 sts, [k1, yo] twice,
k5—10 sts.
Row 8 Bind off 3 sts, p6—7 sts.
Row 9 K3, yo, k1, yo, k3—9 sts.
Row 10 and 12 Purl.
Row 11 K4, yo, k1, yo, k4—11 sts.
Row 13 Bind off 3 sts, k7—8 sts.
Row 14 Bind off 3 sts—5 sts.
Row 15 Ssk, k1, k2tog—3 sts.
Row 16 Purl.
Row 17 SK2P—1 st.
Fasten off.

BERRIES

(make 16)
Cast on 1 st,
Row 1 K in front and back of st.
Row 2 K in front and back of first
st, k1, k in front and back of last
st—5 sts.
Rows 3, 5 and 7 Purl.
Rows 4 and 6 Knit.
Row 8 K2tog, k1, k2tog.
Row 9 P3tog.
Tie cast-on and bind-off tails tog
securely and trim to ½"/1.5cm.

FINISHING

Felt all pieces according to
instructions on p. 8, placing leaves
and berries in a laundry bag. Bowl
is shaped by increases and
decreases but will need reshaping
when wet. Place a hand inside and
a hand outside to shape curve.
Let dry and with large sewing
needle and thread, sew leaves and
berries to rim of bowl as pictured.

techniques

terms & abbreviations

3-needle joining technique Work sts of both layers tog, using 3-needle joining technique as foll: with RS of layers facing (top layer over bottom layer) and the needles parallel, insert a third needle into the first st on each needle and work them tog.

approx approximately

beg begin(ning)

bind off Used to finish an edge and keep stitches from unraveling. Lift the first stitch over the second, the second over the third, etc. (U.K.: cast off)

cast on A foundation row of stitches placed on the needle in order to begin knitting.

cm centimeter(s)

cn cable needle

cont continue(ing)

dec decrease(ing)—Reduce the stitches in a row (knit 2 together).

dpn double pointed needle(s)

foll follow(s)(ing)

g gram(s)

garter stitch Knit every row. Circular knitting: knit one round, then purl one round.

inc increase(ing)—Add stitches in a row (knit into the front and back of a stitch).

k knit

k2tog knit 2 stitches together

kfb knit the front and back loops of the st—2 stitches

LH left-hand

m meter(s)

M1 make one stitch—With the needle tip, lift the strand between last stitch worked and next stitch on the left-hand needle and knit into the back of it. One stitch has been added.

make bobble (MB) Cast on 1 st. K in front, back, front, back and front again of st (5 sts made in one st). Turn. K 1 row, p 1 row, k 1 row. Next Row P2tog, p1, p2tog—3 sts. K 1 row. P3tog, fasten off.

MC main color

p purl

p2 (p3) (p5) tog purl 2 (3) (5) stitches together

pat pattern

pick up and knit (purl) Knit (or purl) into the loops along an edge.

pm place marker—Place or attach a loop of contrast yarn or purchased stitch marker as indicated.

psso pass slipped stitch over

p2sso pass 2 slipped stitches over

rem remain(s)(ing)

rep repeat

rev St st reverse Stockinette stitch—Purl right-side rows, knit wrong-side rows. Circular knitting: purl all rounds. (U.K.: reverse stocking stitch)

rnd(s) round(s)

RH right-hand

RS right side(s)

S2KP Sl 2 sts tog, k1, pass the 2 sl sts over the k1—2 sts dec.

SKP Slip 1, knit 1, pass slip stitch over knit 1.

SK2P Slip 1, knit 2 together, pass slip stitch over k2tog.

sl slip—An unworked stitch made by passing a stitch from the left-hand to the right-hand needle as if to purl.

ssk slip, slip, knit—Slip next 2 stitches knitwise, one at a time, to right-hand needle. Insert tip of left-hand needle into fronts of these stitches from left to right. Knit them together. One stitch has been decreased.

st(s) stitch(es)

St st Stockinette stitch—Knit RS rows, purl WS rows. Circular knitting: knit all rounds. (UK: stocking stitch)

tbl through back of loop

tog together

WS wrong side(s)

wyib with yarn in back

wyif with yarn in front

work even Continue in pattern without increasing or decreasing. (U.K.: work straight)

yd yard(s)

yo yarn over—Make a new stitch by wrapping the yarn over the right-hand needle. (U.K.: yfwd, yon, yrn)

* repeat directions following * as many times as indicated.

[ ] repeat directions inside brackets as many times as indicated.

MAKING CORDS

I-Cord Using dpns or a short circular needle, cast on 3 sts or number of stitches required.

Row 1 K3, do not turn, slide sts to other end of needle.

Rep row 1 to desired length. Bind off.

Twisted cord (used for twisted cord handle) Make I-cord twice as long as desired length. Fold in half. Secure the fold and twist the two ends in the same direction until the cord kinks. Holding both ends in one hand, release the cord, allowing the ends to twist around each other.

provisional cast-on

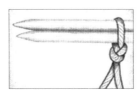

1 This is a cast-on method used when stitches are to be picked up and worked later, such as for hems or special edges. Using two needles held together, begin with a slipknot.

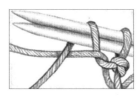

2 Hold a long strand of waste yarn beside the slipknot and take the working yarn under the waste yarn and then behind it again until all stitches are cast on.

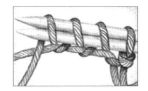

3 Before knitting, withdraw one needle, then knit into the front of the loops on the first row. Leave waste yarn in until you are ready to pick up stitches and add your edge later.

three-needle bind-off

This bind-off is used to join two edges that have the same number of stitches, which have been placed on holders.

1 With the right side of the two pieces facing each other, and the needles parallel, insert a third needle knitwise into the first stitch of each needle. Wrap the yarn around the needle as if to knit.

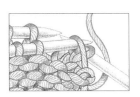

2 Knit these two stitches together and slip them off the needles. *Knit the next two stitches together in the same way as shown.

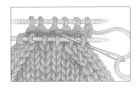

3 Slip the first stitch on the third needle over the second stitch and off the needle. Repeat from the * in step 2 across the row until all the stitches are bound off.

kitchener stitch

1 Insert tapestry needle purlwise (as shown) through first stitch on front needle. Pull yarn through, leaving that stitch on knitting needle.

2 Insert tapestry needle knitwise (as shown) through first stitch on back needle. Pull yarn through, leaving stitch on knitting needle.

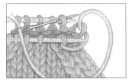

3 Insert tapestry needle knitwise through first stitch on front needle, slip stitch off needle and insert tapestry needle purlwise (as shown) through next stitch on front needle. Pull yarn through, leaving this stitch on needle.

4 Insert tapestry needle purlwise through first stitch on back needle. Slip stitch off needle and insert tapestry needle knitwise (as shown) through next stitch on back needle. Pull yarn through, leaving this stitch on needle.
Repeat steps 3 and 4 until all stitches on both front and back needles have been grafted. Fasten off and weave in end.

duplicate stitch

embroidery stitches

bullion stitch

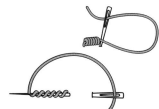

chain stitch

straight stitch

daisy stitch

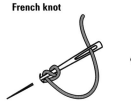

French knot

jacobean couching

leaf stitch

stem stitch

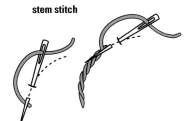

chevron stitch

winter and summer

pointsettia p. 129

sunflower p. 129

spring tulip garden p. 129

Techniques

cut felted flowers p. 130

Techniques

animal friends p. 131

pretty posie p. 132

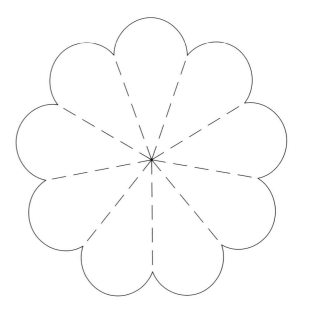

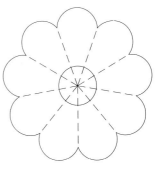

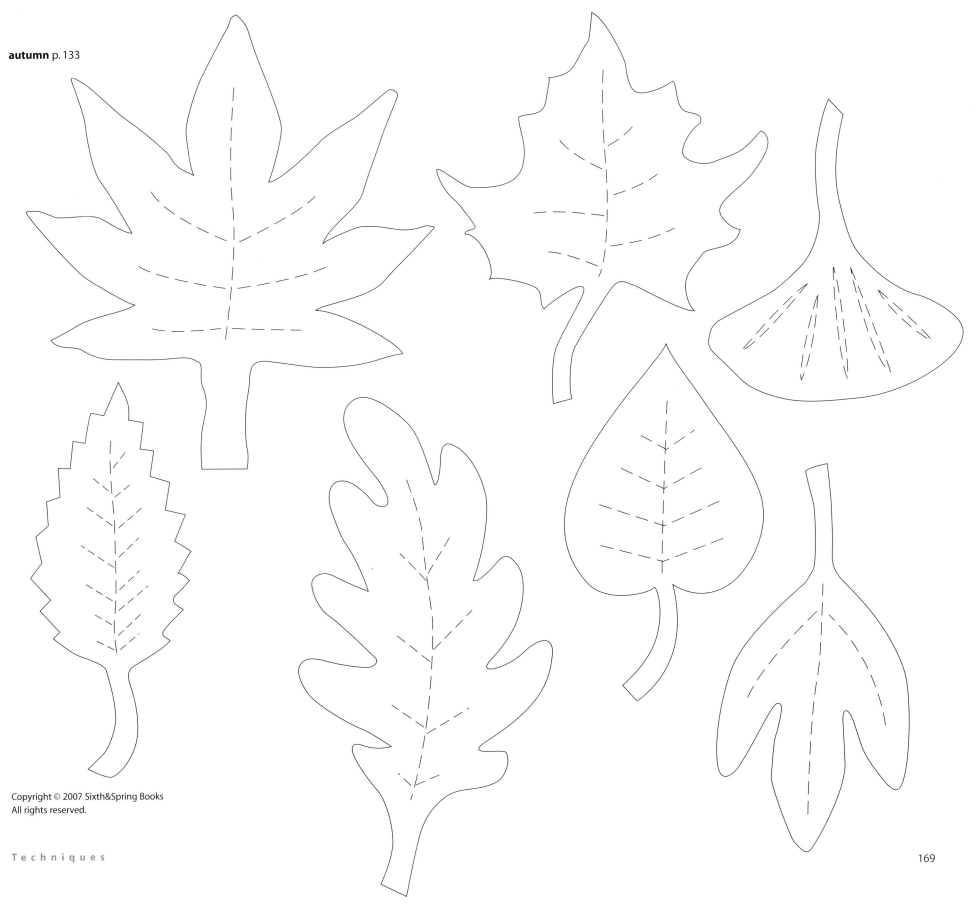

christmas stocking p. 138

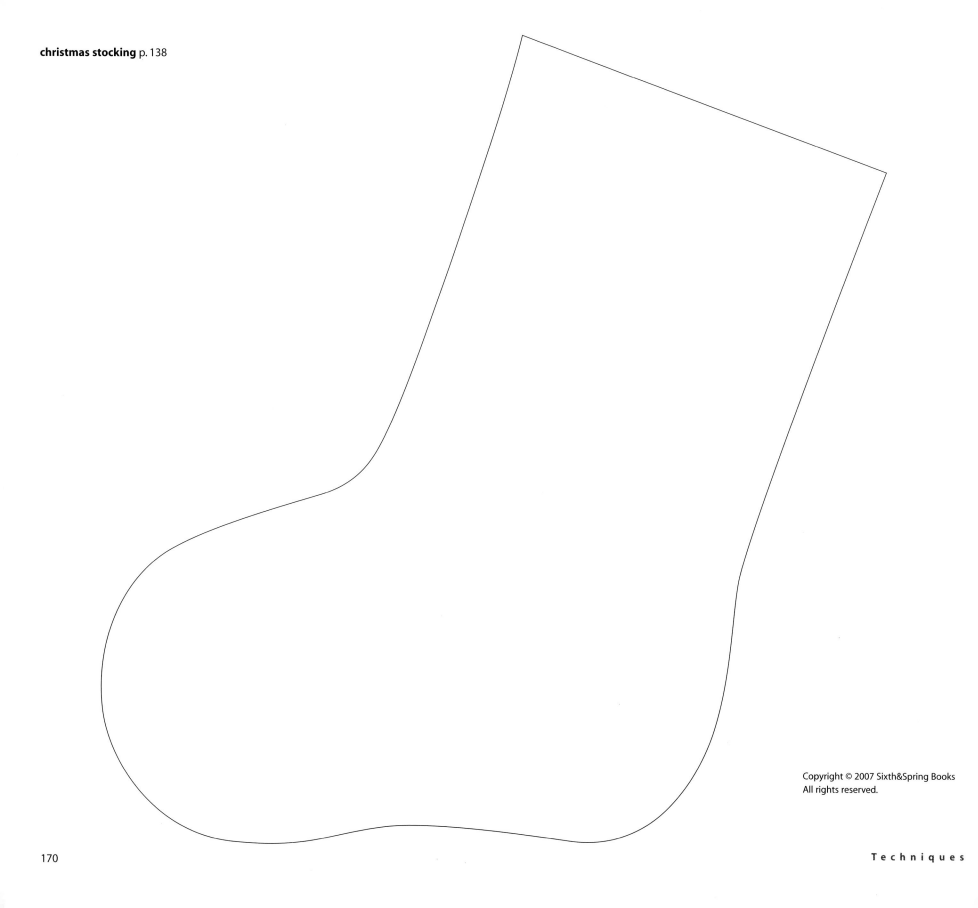

fish p. 141

enlarge 200%

5-in-1 sweater projects pp. 144-145

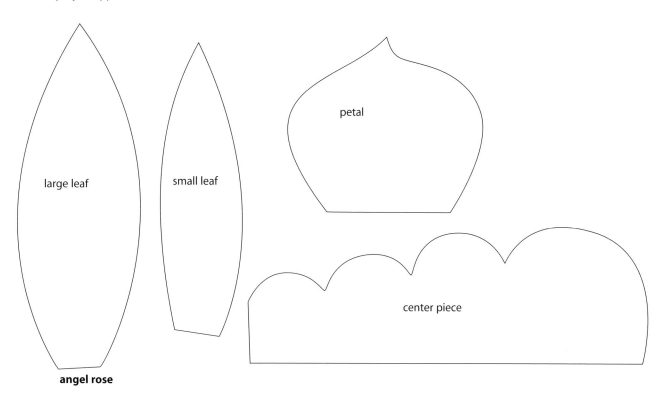

large leaf

small leaf

petal

center piece

angel rose

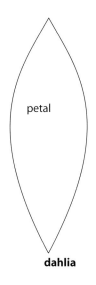

petal

dahlia

notes

notes

acknowledgments

My heartfelt thanks to all the people who helped me on this joyous journey from wool to washing machine to wonderment:

To the intrepid gang at Sixth&Spring Books, who support me all the way: Trisha Malcolm, Elaine Silverstein, Erica Smith, Erin Walsh, Tanis Gray, Eve Ng, Susan Haviland, Marjory Anderson, Sheena Thomas, Adina Klein, Jane Fay and Lillian Esposito.

To my wonderful art director, Chi Ling Moy, whose talent remains unshrinkable, even after felting.

To Jack Deutsch and his staff, whose glorious photography beautifully captured the subtle idiosyncrasies of the felting process.

To my terrific knitters, who burned the midnight oil and some of their husbands' dinners in meeting my deadlines: Eileen Curry, Nancy Henderson, Barbara Kerr, Dianne Weitzul, Margi Hanlon, Patricia Halan, Dana Matursky, Pam Crosson, Meggan Walz, Irene Speir and Martina Browning.

To the generous yarn companies that allowed me to shrink their beautiful yarns: Berroco, Brown Sheep Co., Cascade, Crystal Palace, Harrisville, Lion Brand, Lorna's Laces, Muench, Naturally NZ/Fiber Trends, Patons, Plymouth, Reynolds, Rowan, Takhi•Stacy Charles and Trendsetter.

To my friends, for their never-ending support: Emily Brenner, Jo Brandon, Heris Stenzel (thanks in particular for her organizational skills), Vincent Caputo, Wendy Cheung, Rita Greenfeder, Chris Kitch, David Farrow, Leigh Merrifield, Sonja Dagress and Jenni Stone.

To my website readers and especially whose who shared their felting experiences.

As always, special thanks to my readers, students, designers, knitters and yarn shop owners throughout the world for their expressions of appreciation for my work. Your continuing enthusiasm fuels my creativity.

Finally, many thanks to my husband, Howard, my severest critic and biggest fan.

resources

Berroco, Inc.
P.O. Box 367
14 Elmdale Road
Uxbridge, MA 01569
www.berroco.com

Brown Sheep Company
100662 County Road 16
Mitchell, Nebraska 69357
www.brownsheep.com

Cascade Yarns
1224 Andover Park E.
Tukwila, WA 98188
www.cascadeyarns.com

Crystal Palace Yarns
160 23rd Street
Richmond, CA 94804
www.crystalpalaceyarns.com

Fiber Trends
P.O. Box 7266
E. Wenatchee, WA 98802
www.fibertrends.com

GGH
distributed by
Muench Yarns

Harrisville Designs
41 Main Street
Harrisville, NH 03450
www.harrisville.com

JCA, Inc.
35 Scales Lane
Townsend, MA 01469
www.jcacrafts.com

Lacis
3163 Adeline Street
Berkeley, CA 94703
www.lacis.com

Leisure Arts
5701 Ranch Drive
Little Rock, AR 72223
www.leisurearts.com

Lion Brand Yarn
34 West 15th Street
New York, NY 10011
www.lionbrand.com

Lorna's Laces
4229 North Honore Street
Chicago, IL 60613
www.lornaslaces.net

Muench Yarns, Inc.
1323 Scott Street
Petaluma, CA 94954
www.myyarns.com

Nashua Handknits
distributed by
Westminster Fibers, Inc.

Naturally NZ
15 Church Street
Onehunga
Auckland, New Zealand
www.naturallyyarnsnz.com
U.S.: distributed by
Fiber Trends
Canada: distributed by
The Old Mill Knitting Company

The Old Mill Knitting Company
P.O. Box 81176
Ancaster, Ontario
Canada L9G 4X2
www.oldmillknitting.com

Patons Yarns
320 Livingstone Avenue South
Listowel, Ontario
Canada N4W 3H3
www.patonsyarns.com

Plymouth Yarn Company
P.O. Box 28
Bristol, PA 19007
www.plymouthyarn.com

Reynolds
distributed by
JCA, Inc.

Rowan Yarns
distributed by
Westminster Fibers, Inc.
U.K.:
Green Lane Mill
Holmfirth
HD9 2DX England
www.knitrowan.com

Sunbelt Fastener
8841 Exposition Boulevard
Culver City, CA 90230
www.sunbeltfastener.com

Tahki•Stacy Charles, Inc.
70-30 80th Street
Building #36
Ridgewood, NY 11385
www.tahkistacycharles.com

Trendsetter Yarns
16745 Saticoy Street
Suite #101
Van Nuys, CA 91406
www.trendsetteryarns.com
Canada:
distributed by
The Old Mill Knitting Company

Westminster Fibers
4 Townsend West, Unit 8
Nashua, NH 03063
www.westminsterfibers.com